OCT   2012

OVER-THE-RHINE

OVER-THE-RHINE
WHEN BEER WAS KING
★

Michael D. Morgan

Charleston   London

THE
History
PRESS

Published by The History Press
Charleston, SC 29403
www.historypress.net

Unless otherwise noted, all images are from the author's collection.

First published 2010
Second printing 2011
Third printing 2012

Manufactured in the United States
ISBN 978.1.59629.914.6

Library of Congress Cataloging-in-Publication Data
Morgan, Michael D.
Over-the-Rhine : when beer was king / Michael D. Morgan.
p. cm.
Includes bibliographical references.
ISBN 978-1-59629-914-6
1. Over-the-Rhine (Cincinnati, Ohio)--History. 2. Cincinnati (Ohio)--History. 3. Over-the-Rhine (Cincinnati, Ohio)--Social conditions. 4. Cincinnati (Ohio)--Social conditions. 5. Beer--Ohio--Cincinnati--History. 6. Breweries--Ohio--Cincinnati--History. 7. Drinking of alcoholic beverages--Ohio--Cincinnati--History. 8. German Americans--Ohio--Cincinnati--History. 9. Over-the-Rhine (Cincinnati, Ohio)--Ethnic relations. 10. Cincinnati (Ohio)--Ethnic relations. I. Title.
F499.C56O846 2010
977.1'78--dc22
2010030905

For Amy. Thank you for your help, patience, support and love through this book and all of the Over-the-Rhine years.

CONTENTS

FOREWORD

My history with Cincinnati beer started as a young beer representative for a distributor that serviced the Athens, Ohio market. While I was working for that distributor and selling Cincinnati beer, I just happened to be in the city to watch one of the last days of production at the old Hudepohl brewery on Gest Street. I watched those bottles roll off the line and I saw the faces of the people around me, and the sense of loss was heartbreaking. Even though I wasn't from here, I understood what they were feeling. Beer is a huge part of the city's history. When Cincinnati lost local ownership of its brands, I felt like it was losing a big part of its soul as a city, and I bought the Christian Moerlein, Hudepohl, Burger, Schoenling, Little Kings and over sixty other local brands both to build a business and to try to do the right thing for Cincinnati—to bring back its brewing heritage.

After I met Mike Morgan during Bockfest 2006 and learned more about the history of the Brewery District in Over-the-Rhine, I started to get increasingly interested in the neighborhood because most of the brands I now own came from there. I already planned on bringing the Cincinnati brewing heritage back to town, but as I learned more about the history of Over-the-Rhine and started getting involved in its revitalization, I knew that there was one place above all others where Moerlein and Hudepohl should be brewed. It had to be their original home—Over-the-Rhine. A lot of very smart, suburban advisers tried to steer me in other directions, but I knew that I wanted to be part of the neighborhood's future. I wanted to authentically restore Over-the-Rhine's brewing heritage.

My commitment to Over-the-Rhine started by learning about its history. That's what brings it alive. That's what makes you understand what is so important about saving and rebuilding it. In the time that I have been involved in Over-the-Rhine, I have seen very few people who are as committed to the neighborhood, as knowledgeable about its history or as passionate about sharing it as Mike Morgan. He has been essential in both inspiring me and helping me bring Cincinnati's brewing heritage back to the city, and I'm glad that he has made his contribution to telling this early history of Over-the-Rhine.

Greg Hardman
President and CEO
Christian Moerlein Brewing Co.

ACKNOWLEDGEMENTS

In late 2005, I found myself in the usual position at the bar at Arnold's Bar & Grill, but I also found myself in the extremely *un*usual position of agreeing to organize a parade for an event called Bockfest. This began a very long journey into the rich history of Over-the-Rhine and led to a compulsion to save it from destruction. Part of this work has included sharing the neighborhood's story with others, because the first step in preventing Over-the-Rhine from physical destruction is to help people understand why it is worth saving. It is valuable from a purely architectural standpoint, but it is more than that. It is a living and endangered piece of American history. As I shared Over-the-Rhine's story through tours and public presentations, I became cognizant of the questions that I couldn't answer because I couldn't find those answers in any of the numerous publications about either Over-the-Rhine or Cincinnati's brewing history. This is not a book about brewing history. That has already been done. It also does not claim to be a complete history of Over-the-Rhine or even an exhaustive chronicle of its earliest years. This is a book about the early history of Over-the-Rhine that attempts to answer the questions that I could not previously answer about the role of beer, brewing and German ethnicity in the rise and fall of Over-the-Rhine.

I owe a debt of gratitude to Steven Hampton, president of the Brewery District CURC, both for his assistance with this publication as well as all that he does for Over-the-Rhine; and to Greg Hardman, president and CEO of Christian Moerlein Brewing Company and the caretaker and redeemer of Cincinnati's brewing heritage. While I have known both of these men for only a few years, they have been Over-the-Rhine years, which are much longer than standard human years and require good, trusted friends to survive with sanity.

Thanks to Chris Smith, Diane Mallstrom, David Siders and many other members of the exceptional staff in the Public Library of Cincinnati.

I am also grateful to Linda Bailey of the Cincinnati Museum Center and Kevin Grace of the University of Cincinnati for their assistance with historic photographs.

Most of all, thanks to my wife, Amy, for all of her assistance. I could not have completed this project without her.

HOW TO FIND A BUILDING UNDER YOUR BUILDING

On a mid-November morning in 2009, an architect, two lawyers and the president of a beer company stood on a section of McMicken Avenue sidewalk arguing about the dates and order of events that led to the repeal of Prohibition. Over the past few decades, the streets of Cincinnati's Over-the-Rhine have gained a reputation for a number of activities. Spontaneous academic debate is not one of them, but this group of amateur local historians was waiting to see what a couple of amateur urban archaeologists were going to find underneath the sidewalk in front of them.

The backhoe was two hours late, but eventually the large diesel truck pulled up, dropped its loading ramps and started backing a large piece of excavation equipment onto McMicken. Dump truck and backhoe assumed their positions, hurricane fencing was wrapped around a tree and some poles to block off sidewalk traffic, the small group of onlookers stopped arguing and assumed a safe distance and the dump bucket made a multiton tap onto the sidewalk's concrete surface. Roughly ten minutes later, the backhoe firmly snagged its claws on a sheet of broken concrete, lifting one edge a couple feet from the surface. Everything stopped. The operator climbed down from the equipment. The onlookers moved forward. The mystery of what lay underneath was about to be revealed.

In most city neighborhoods, pulling back a piece of concrete to look underneath it would involve a lot less suspense. In most places, the decision to pay several thousand dollars to unload heavy equipment onto a downtown street for the purpose of ripping up the sidewalk—without a permit—could be viewed as proof of mental instability, but Over-the-Rhine is not most places. Building owners Doug and Mike Bootes may be the first to call this adventure in urban excavation a little crazy, but it was also based on recent discoveries, a series of mathematical calculations and a gnawing mystery that anybody with a good sense of curiosity should understand.

Mike Bootes lives in one of five buildings that used to be part of a commercial brewing complex. The Bauer Brewery was founded on the site in 1865. It changed hands and operated for only a year as the George Bach Brewery in 1874 and then was sold and became Schmidt and Prell Brewery in 1876. It stayed with members of the Schmidt family, subsequently becoming Schmidt and Brother Brewery and Schmidt Brothers Brewing Company, until it was sold in 1905. For its remaining life as a brewery, it was known as Crown Brewery, named after the Crown Beer that had been the brewery's staple product during the Schmidt years. The brewery never became one of the city's largest, but the different eras and architectural styles of its buildings show its expansion over time, and it stayed in business roughly sixty-one years. The brewery was composed of two connected buildings on the north side of McMicken (including the Booteses' residence) and three connected buildings on the south side (all three on the south are connected and referred to collectively as "the south building").

The Schmidt Brothers Brewery had several features common to Cincinnati's nineteenth-century breweries. The location on opposite sides of the street is both inconvenient and almost universal. The federal government imposed a tax on beer production to help pay for the Civil War, but unlike previous alcohol taxes, this one stayed in place and its terms became burdensome when breweries started to make bottled beer a more significant part of their businesses in the 1870s and 1880s. The tax levied one dollar on each barrel. As a number of innovations were making bottling much more feasible in the 1880s, the required means of paying the tax was still a stamp that had to be physically placed on the barrel itself. "Barrel" wasn't just a measurement of volume; it meant an actual wooden barrel full of beer. Afraid that bottling would circumvent the tax, the law required that bottling facilities be separated from the brew house, with no physical connection. In 1890, somebody—and many sources speculate that the "somebody" was Frederick Pabst—convinced members of Congress to change the law. New processes for gauging and monitoring volume were imposed, and it became legal to connect the brew house to bottling facilities with a pipeline.

The south portion of Schmidt Brewery as it appears today at 133 East McMicken Avenue. These three buildings illustrate changes in ownership and expansion ranging from the establishment of the Bauer Brewery in 1865, through Schmidt family ownership between 1870 and 1905, through the demise of Crown Brewery during Prohibition.

At its peak, Over-the-Rhine was home to tens of thousands of people. It was the center of German-American culture in Cincinnati and also became home to the seedier side of the city's social and political life. It was home to hundreds of saloons. For most of the nineteenth century, the neighborhood had over a dozen breweries operating in or near its borders and dozens of ancillary businesses that served brewing and the saloon trade, as well as hundreds of other businesses and industries. Over-the-Rhine was one of the most densely populated neighborhoods in America, and it would have been hard to move around in. Trying to operate a business by constantly crossing a street full of people, horses, wagons and early motor vehicles would have been challenging, and McMicken was a major artery, once serving as the primary road heading west out of town. Imagine the modern equivalent of having to leave your office and push a cart full of paper and supplies across a busy city street every time you needed to make copies. That's what moving keg beer across the street to bottle it must have felt like, so breweries with any degree of bottling capacity dug connecting tunnels when the law permitted them to do so.

The proliferation of breweries and saloons in Over-the-Rhine was driven in large part by the creation and proliferation of a new type of beer called "lager" in the mid-1800s. Lager required a longer brewing process. In fact, the term "lager" is a derivative of a German word meaning "to store." This type of beer also required cool temperatures. Prior to artificial refrigeration, breweries needed a way to keep lager beer chilled during brewing. The most common answer to creating a chilled environment without electricity was to dig cavernous subbasements that either went thirty to forty feet underground or back into McMicken's steep hillside to reach cavelike conditions. These arched cavernous rooms, called "lagering cellars" or the German "felsen" tunnels, created a roughly constant fifty-five-degree environment. Copper pipes run along the walls and ceilings of lagering cellars circulated brine, ammonia or cold water in a crude, early version of air conditioning to bring temperatures down to about forty degrees. When the brewing complexes could be connected, breweries built tunnels underneath the city streets (below sewer or municipal waterlines) connecting their subterranean chambers.

Iron and steel brackets remain rusting in the humid subbasements. Brackets would have originally held lines carrying chilled water to help refrigerate the lagering cellars. The bracket pictured may also have carried beer lines from the brew house to the bottling facility. No piping remains in any of the known lagering cellars, probably reused decades ago.

After its demise, the Crown Brewery was devoted to other commercial uses. It became a plumbing supply company and a decorative plaster manufacturer. Lagering cellars had a number of air shafts to regulate humidity and holes for piping beer between different parts of the brewing process. When the breweries ceased to be used as breweries, the cellars and tunnels were closed, and almost all of them were sealed in the intervening years, just leaving holes in basement floors leading to "nowhere." It became common practice to use these entrances to the subterranean Over-the-Rhine as garbage holes, which is what both the plaster business and plumbing supply business did with them. The plumbing company started chucking broken and discarded fixtures down a large opening that led from the first floor, through the basement, to the subbasement lagering cellars below. Over the years, the subbasement chamber at the bottom of this hole accumulated a mountain of broken porcelain, which reached to the top of the chamber and blocked entrance to the subbasement. Throughout most of the neighborhood, these subbasements were sealed entirely, which was the approach taken by the former owners of Mike Bootes's property, leaving an intriguing cinder block arch in the side of his stone basement wall.

Ted Love bought the Schmidt Brothers southern building in the summer of 2008. Love succumbed to his curiosity rather quickly and hired a crew of laborers to remove the discarded plumbing parts from the entrance to his subbasement. Hauling out construction dumpsters full of porcelain allowed Love and his crew to become the first people to walk into the subterranean lagering caverns in decades. The exploration also revealed an oval, stone tunnel that exits the subbasement chambers and travels under McMicken Avenue to the Bootes property. At basement level, the crew also broke through a brick wall into an arched room immediately under the sidewalk but sealed and forgotten for at least a generation.

On the other side of the street, Mike Bootes started poking holes in his mysterious cinder block arch. Ted Love's crew had removed bricks and found vacant, empty space. Mike's experience was different: a torrent of loose fill started pouring into his basement. Mike, his brother Doug and the friends that they had gathered to celebrate Doug's birthday by smashing a hole in their basement wall stood back and watched a seemingly endless river of dirt, gravel, broken bricks and small pieces of concrete flood out of the hole and onto the floor. They waited. They drank some beer. They waited, and hours later a trickle of fill was still tumbling out of the hole. Someone finally asked, "I wonder if the sidewalk will collapse?" Good question. Nobody knew the answer.

Ted Love's tunnel under McMicken ended in a pile of bricks, roughly ten feet away from and fifteen feet below Mike Bootes's dirt-spewing archway. What lay between, and how these spaces connected, remained unknown. Less curious people might have cleaned up their basement floor, patched the hole and lived a happy life with that mystery remaining unsolved, but neither Mike nor Doug Bootes is one of those people. The curiosity drove them to hire a backhoe to start pounding a hole in a Cincinnati sidewalk.

As the backhoe claw lifted its first sheet of sidewalk, the crowd moved forward to look into the hole. It was clear that the sidewalk had been poured on forms atop very old steel beams and that at least part of the space underneath was hollow, but it was also full of dirt and brick fill. Bootes made the call: "Keep digging." Forty-eight hours and a lot of work later, a roughly twenty- by ten-foot chamber under the sidewalk— or, more accurately, where the sidewalk *used* to be—had been completely excavated. The chamber essentially mirrored the one at basement level across the street, with one significant difference. As the last of the fill was shoveled off the floor by hand, the top of a graceful stone arch started to become visible at the bottom of the basement wall. The area in front of it showed a cut in the stone floor filled with loose, sandy soil. Obviously, this was the filled-in entrance to whatever space connected the tunnel under McMicken to some area below Mike Bootes's brand-new yet over one-hundred-year-old basement addition, but there was still an unknown area separating several feet in distance and about fifteen feet down. The stairs could lead straight to the tunnel, or they could lead to another subbasement chamber where the tunnel connected. This question would have to simmer a little longer.

City of Cincinnati staff are, on occasion, accused of diligence. It was on one such occasion that a building inspector utilized his expertly trained eyes and professional knowledge to conclude that there was something amiss about the fact that a twenty-foot piece of sidewalk on a downtown street had been replaced over the weekend by a fifteen-foot-deep hole, surrounded by bright orange hurricane fence. (Taxpaying Cincinnatians might want to believe that staff in a lesser city would have missed this subtle irregularity.) So Mike Bootes obtained the appropriate permits, engineering and architectural documentation, etc. and spent the next several weeks replacing the sidewalk.

Workers inside the Crown Brewery in the early twentieth century. This photo appears to have been taken in the northern half of the brewery, in the building that currently houses Superior Rubber. *Courtesy of Steven Hampton, president, Brewery District CURC.*

On New Year's Eve 2010, over a dozen volunteers gathered in Mike Bootes's basement with shovels, buckets and a bunch of beer with a mission to connect the Bootes property with the McMicken tunnel somewhere roughly fifteen feet below. Alternately taking turns in the hole where the stairwell used to be, a crew more accustomed to manning bar stools at Murphy's Pub did the backbreaking work of passing bucket after bucket of dirt and stone out of the hole. An assembly line system of beer laborers got wheelbarrows full of debris upstairs and pushed them down Hust Alley to a vacant lot. As drug dealers on East Clifton watched this constant procession going up and down the alley, undoubtedly wondering what kind of weird New Year's Eve celebration this might be, the crew in the basement broke through to the other side a few hours before the end of 2009.

What's most interesting about the Schmidt Brothers excavation is not that a guy would become so overwhelmed by curiosity that he would haul tons of broken porcelain out of a subbasement before patching his roof, or that the same motivation would cause his neighbor to start ripping up a city sidewalk without permission. What's most interesting is that the Schmidt Brothers story has precedent, and it is unlikely to be the last subterranean world rediscovered in Over-the-Rhine.

Chris Frutkin and Fred Berger bought a building that used to be part of the Kauffman Brewery in the late nineteenth and early twentieth centuries. Chris and Fred are both in the real estate development, rental and management business, and they bought the building in the early 1990s to convert the industrial space to loft apartments.

The real estate agent who sold Chris and Fred the building had also sold it to previous owners. About a year after the sale to Chris and Fred, the agent decided to retire and was cleaning out old files. In the file from the 1956 sale of the property, he found architectural drawings of the Kauffman brew house (not copies, but the original architectural drawings from the 1880s construction). The agent was thoughtful enough to give the copies to Chris. As he looked them over, he became more intrigued by what the plans showed. Neither Chris nor Fred is an architect, but they have both been around enough development to be able to read architectural drawings, and even someone who lacks this skill can identify the fact that the drawings showed an additional floor to the building that was no longer known to exist. At first, they assumed that plans had changed during construction; but upon closer examination, another possibility emerged.

Chris went down to the basement with a sledgehammer and knocked a hole through a sealed archway. In most basements, this would lead to dirt. In Chris's, it led to a tunnel that wrapped around the sides of his basement and that had been sealed for decades. Exploration continued. In the tunnel, Chris found a hole. In the hole, Chris found an extra eleven-thousand-square-foot building that he didn't know he owned—below the basement.

John Kauffman's Vine Street brewery was one of the more successful in the city. It opened in 1860, rose to be the fourth largest in the city by 1871 and remained in business until Prohibition shut it down in 1919. The brewery had two tunnels connecting it to part of the brewery complex on Hamer Street, behind Vine, one at basement level and one at the subbasement level that Chris found when he crawled through a hole in his basement in about 1994.

The Kauffman brewery building story illustrates a uniquely Over-the-Rhine phenomenon. Where else can you find an eleven-thousand-square-foot building underneath your building? The portion of the former Kauffman brewery on Hamer Street was best known to Cincinnatians for decades as the Husman Potato Chip factory. The tunnel under Hamer Street leads to five subbasement felsen tunnels underneath the former Husman factory. Structural and environmental analysis of the building done during Husman's ownership is free of any mention of these tunnels, suggesting that the company operated there for decades with no knowledge that it owned thousands of square feet of building underneath its basement.

Subbasement cellars were used for more than beer production. The Kauffman brewery also built a large apartment building for workers at 1725 Vine Street that contains large subbasement cellars that were used for beer storage. Providing free or reduced-rate rent to workers was a typical part of nineteenth-century brewery employment, and other breweries owned housing. Many of the lagering cellars and tunnels became obsolete while the breweries were still in operation because of the advent of artificial refrigeration in the mid-1880s. In subsequent years, the spaces would have been of limited use, and after Prohibition they would have been little more than a liability—particularly in residential properties. When different parts of brewing complexes were sold to different owners, it would have been undesirable to have tunnels connecting them. There is also speculation that some of the cellars and tunnels were used to produce and transport beer during Prohibition. Although this is unsubstantiated, it makes sense. What better place for an underground brewing operation than literally underground—in space constructed for the purpose of brewing? For all of these reasons, Over-the-Rhine's underworld was sealed off, forgotten and may have been intentionally hidden during the 1920s.

Cincinnati's brewing industry didn't fade away. It was forced to an abrupt halt, and a lot of brewery real estate was sold in the first few years after Prohibition as the businesses folded and the corporations dissolved. The past was literally sealed under basements and through bricked or blocked-up stone archways by a generation of people who are almost entirely gone. As a result, these spaces continue to be found. When the Alms and Doepke Park Haus garage was built at the corner of Reading and Sycamore, filling in the massive lagering cellars under the demolished site of the Gambrinus Stock Brewery in a way that would have supported heavy construction above was so daunting that it was easier to build concrete piers to the bottom of the former brewery's subbasement and construct the five-story parking garage on top of them. Even many known spaces contain unknowns. A subbasement under part of the former Sohn Brewery on Stonewall

George Weber's Jackson Brewery as it appears today.

and Mohawk Streets is open, but an artesian well at the bottom and a deteriorated ladder have left the space unexplored for decades; and stories persist of unfound and extensive tunnel networks. Former Jackson Brewery building owner Denny Dellinger was told by stewards of the building decades earlier that they had found tunnels exiting the building's massive lagering cellars and traveling so far that they turned back before they found an end. Dellinger, an architect, was unable to find these legendary tunnels but says that the original architectural drawings for the building indicate that they might exist and a number of archway patterns in the stone walls raise the question of whether doorways were sealed with stone in the years intervening between the fabled journey through an extensive tunnel and Dellinger's twenty-first-century purchase.

The Jackson Brewery tunnel legend is probably just an urban Cincinnati myth, but it is also very likely that there are subterranean spaces in Over-the-Rhine that remain unexplored by a living generation. Brewery buildings have also contained other odd discoveries. The Christian Moerlein Brewery's Old Jug Lager pottery bottles are a plentiful and amazingly well-preserved local collectible because about five thousand of them were found in brand-new condition in the former bottling building decades after the end of

Cases of unused crockery bottles of Moerlein's Old Jug lager were found stored in the depths of the former Christian Moerlein bottling building in new condition almost one hundred years after their production.

Prohibition; and a room in the basement of the former John Hauck Brewery office is still full of nineteenth-century bottling corks.

Thousands of intervening years, climate changes and shifting sands make it easy to understand how pharaohs' tombs get lost in the Egyptian desert, but how do you completely lose eleven thousand square feet of building underneath a building, in the heart of an American city, that was used less than one hundred years ago? The answer lies in how a distinct American subculture and one of the city—and nation's—most important industries were both brought to an abrupt end. The answer is the relatively sudden, unexpected death of a place in time that existed over Cincinnati's "Rhine."

WHISKEY, PIGS AND ADULTEROUS LUST
Birth of a City

A schoolteacher, war hero, lawyer, congressman and former chief justice of New Jersey named John Cleves Symmes extended his lengthy résumé to include surveyor and speculator and purchased a huge tract of land in southwest Ohio. He advertised the land for sale in quarters and sold all of what is now Hamilton County to a fellow New Jerseyan named Mathias Denmann in 1788. The roughly seven to eight hundred acres that became nineteenth-century Cincinnati was purchased for $500. Denmann met up with a Colonel Patterson and a Kentucky schoolteacher named Filson in the town of Maysville (then named Limestone), divided the land up into thirds and hatched a plan to build a city. They teamed up with Symmes and two other surveyors named McMillan and Ludlow and left Maysville on Christmas Eve 1788. The men later disagreed about whether they reached their destination in December 1788 or January 1789, but somewhere in this period of time they disembarked, broke up into two teams and began exploring and surveying their new city—a place that they named Losantiville.

The city was laid out in the Philadelphia method, meaning that it was surveyed and streets were mapped in evenly separated squares with north–south and east–west streets intersecting at ninety-degree angles. While the city's central business district still retains most of the streets from the original survey, this creates a deceptive image about what the early settlement looked like. The streets existed only on a map. The city was a thick, old-growth forest, and this tidy plan of perpendicular streets began with notches on trees. In fact, one of the earliest families had so much difficulty determining

Cincinnati was planned using the Philadelphia method, meaning that it was divided into equal-sized blocks and right angles. Streets were laid out in forest and meadows in essentially the same configuration that still exists today in the central business district. *From the collection of the Public Library of Cincinnati and Hamilton County.*

where the street was supposed to be that they accidentally built their house in the middle of it.

Early life in Losantiville was hard. Food was scarce, the forests were dense and the Shawnee tribe had some pretty pointed questions about why a few dozen white people were cutting down trees on their land. The food situation was addressed mostly by fishing. The Indian situation was a little more complicated. Judge Symmes responded to the Shawnee chief's concerns by showing him a copy of the government documents giving Symmes title to the land. Rather than being pacified by this legalistic approach, the chief fixated on the U.S. government's seal. From his perspective, the spread wings of the eagle in flight and the bundle of arrows in his talon sent a very clear message: war.

At the end of the Revolutionary War, Congress adopted the position that its treaty with Great Britain concluded both England's claim to title of American lands as well as that of all the Indian tribes that had fought with Britain against the American colonists. England surrendered the land claims of six Indian nations, including the Miami, Shawnee and Delaware, all tribes inhabiting the areas around Cincinnati; but the English ceded these claims without the knowledge or consent of the Indian nations. From the Native American perspective, the English and colonists had placed them between a rock and a hard place. They faced retribution from the English if they failed to intervene on the side of Great Britain and were considered to have lost their ancestral lands when England lost the war; yet tribes that managed to stay neutral in the Revolution were subsequently slaughtered by American pioneers with equal malice. This made living in Losantiville dangerous. Leaving the clustered settlement to tend farms or hunt often ended in execution. Early municipal law required citizens to take their firearms with them when attending church. The city nevertheless began to grow from its original eleven families and twenty-four single men. In 1790, Losantiville's population increased by forty families, but growth was marginalized somewhat by twenty citizens being killed in Indian attacks. In 1791, despite new arrivals, the population remained static largely due to the number of people killed fighting Indians. For many years after settlement, the only place safe from Indian attack was within the walls of Losantiville's Fort Washington, and the city may not have survived without the fort.

Cincinnati's location on a bend in the Ohio River and the confluence of several smaller waterways is often noted for the strategic decision to

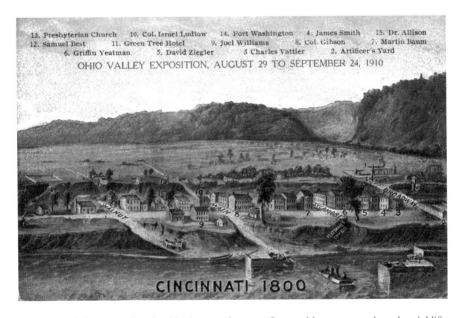

The original city was only a few blocks near the waterfront, with most growth and social life emanating from Fort Washington, located roughly at the corner of Broadway and Third. *From the collection of the Public Library of Cincinnati and Hamilton County.*

make it the site of Fort Washington. However, the real reason for the fort's location may be attributable to a very nonmilitary strategy. The fort was originally supposed to be located in North Bend, Ohio, a river town that is roughly fifteen miles west of downtown Cincinnati. Major Doughty was sent from Marietta to establish the fort at this strategic location. The arrival of Doughty's three hundred troops brought a sense of security to North Bend that attracted a handful of settlers. Among them was a man who apparently had a very attractive wife. While on patrol one day, the major spotted the wife and became quite smitten. Major Doughty must have been relatively bold about his desire, because the woman's husband packed them up and moved to Cincinnati to thwart the major's indecent intentions. This solution proved far more temporary than Doughty's lust. Shortly after the husband and wife left for Losantiville, the officer decided that North Bend was completely unfit for a fort and that the budding settlement of Losantiville was far more appropriate, so he packed up three hundred troops to chase after another man's wife. A nineteenth-century account of the events reflects the randomness of how one man's adulterous desires changed the fate of Cincinnati:

> *The beauty of one female settler shifted Ohio's center of trade from its original cradle to the place where it is now. Had the beauty with her fiery eyes remained in North Bend, then the barracks and fort would have arisen there, North Bend would have become the center of the population, capital of business, and Cincinnati would have been an area of relatively little significance.*

Fort Washington came to be erected near the banks of the river in November 1789. (It was located roughly where Fort Washington Way meets I-471, unceremoniously sitting where two parking garages and an interstate highway now reside.) Without the troops, North Bend held little attraction to the few remaining settlers, and the site was completely deserted within three years after their departure. Although North Bend's panoramic river view eventually led to the settlement of a quaint little town that produced both William Henry Harrison (the ninth U.S. president) and Benjamin Harrison (the twenty-third U.S. president), it never quite recovered from the 1789 amorous departure of its fort. The 2000 U.S. Census reports the population of North Bend as 603 people. Conversely, the location of Fort Washington in Cincinnati helped transform it into the Queen City of the West.

On January 12, 1790, Ohio's governor St. Clair arrived in Lostantiville to organize the local government. Hamilton County got its name from Alexander Hamilton, then the secretary of the treasury, and the governor changed the name of the city to Cincinnati. The name came from the governor's association with the Society of the Cincinnati, a fraternal society founded by Revolutionary War officers to "maintain inviolable those noble human rights and freedoms" for which they "fought and spilled their blood."

The early city grew largely along the riverfront with steep bluffs behind it, and its economy grew from the river as a trading hub. The city saw its first riverboat traffic in 1811, dramatically increasing the speed with which it could connect to ports as far and as economically important as New Orleans. Construction on the Miami and Erie Canal began in 1825, and the Cincinnati connection was completed in November 1828, with the first boats floating down the route that follows Central Parkway in the spring of 1829. At the time, the area east of the canal on its southern route and north of the area after it took a bend at Plum Street where it roughly cut the downtown basin in half was almost entirely vacant land. There were garden plots and a few streets running north–south (and none running east–west), and the area where Washington Park and Music Hall now sit was home to three cemeteries: the park was home to two, segregated by Presbyterian and Episcopalian; and a "public burying ground" was on the Music Hall lot. This was the countryside, the far edge of town.

The canal connected the Great Lakes to the Ohio River and all the farmland in between. It was the first network for interstate commerce, and the combination of the canalboats and riverboats made Cincinnati the most important city in the western lands, a place that could compete with older, eastern seaboard cities. Cincinnati's real estate values rose between 20 and 25 percent in the three years following the completion of the canal; and export trade increased from $1 million in 1826 to $4 million in 1832. Nicholas Longworth's foresight in 1810 to buy thirty acres of what would become the heart of the city helped make him one of the richest men in America by 1830.

The Queen City of the West traded in almost all major commodities of the day, but some staples stood out. Corn was a very common crop grown in the large swaths of farmland served by the canal system, but because it was bulky and plentiful it was also a bad commodity to sell as an export. Instead, farmers either used it to raise pigs or distilled it into whiskey. In

Canal traffic through Cincinnati began in 1828. *From the collection of the Public Library of Cincinnati and Hamilton County.*

1829, pork was the city's key export and bacon was the second (apparently distinguishing between livestock and…bacon). Together, the value of pork and bacon exports was $702,796. By comparison, only $182,236 worth of whiskey was exported. This early boon to the economy produced by swine gave the city its "Porkopolis" nickname, but forgetting the importance of whiskey is a bit of revisionist history. Pork was the king of the early Cincinnati economy, but whiskey had a threefold advantage. First, whiskey doesn't die, get diseased or spoil en route. Second, whiskey doesn't smell like a pig. And third, it will get you drunk. These advantages helped make whiskey a much larger export than pork in the coming decades. By 1881, the value of all forms of livestock passing through the city was $26,000,000 compared to the $30,972,000 in whiskey exports. A decade later, roughly $9,000,000 more whiskey was being exported than all types of livestock combined, and the export value of whiskey and beer together had reached $39,300,000.

The explosion of trade and growth of the city also drew newcomers and created a rapidly changing face of the city. A German family was among one of the first eleven families to settle in Cincinnati and German-American major David Ziegler was elected the city's first mayor in 1802, but Germans were a minority in early Cincinnati. In fact, some historians have attributed Major Ziegler's election, in part, to a sympathetic public reaction to his ethnic-related mistreatment in the army. Ziegler resigned from the army while serving as the commander of Fort Washington due to charges of insubordination and "drunkenness," an early taste of conflicting social mores about alcohol consumption. Most of Cincinnati's early settlers were native born, coming from New Jersey, Pennsylvania and New York. This remained the case for some time. By 1825, 80 percent of the population was still American-born, and people from England, Scotland and Wales constituted a clear majority of foreign-born. That changed as German and Irish immigrants started arriving in significant numbers in the 1830s and 1840s.

In May 1832, tens of thousands of would-be revolutionaries of all walks of life met at Hambach Castle in Rhineland-Palatinate (now one of the sixteen states in Germany) to listen to speeches about liberty and civil rights. Apparently more like Woodstock than storming the Bastille, no cohesive action arose from the festival. In fact, the primary result was a further crackdown on civil liberties and persecution of attendees. This drove many to leave and seek freedom in America. Most of these immigrants were leaving for both political and economic reasons, but enough were well-educated and skilled craftsmen that they became successful professionals, artisans and tradesmen in their new homeland. Its growth and importance on the western frontier made Cincinnati a logical place to come, and immigrants arriving in the 1830s and '40s started changing the face of the city—both its ethnic makeup as well as its physical development. The earliest German immigrants to arrive in the city mixed with the rest of the population along the river and the central business district, but this wave of immigrants known as the "Thirtyers" started to settle in the previously vacant lands north of the canal.

By 1840, immigrants were still living in different areas throughout the small city, but clear development and housing patterns were starting to emerge. In 1842, a large area of field and scrub brush north of the canal and east of Sycamore Street that Cincinnatians called "Texas" was sold off as developable parcels of land, giving birth to the area known as Pendleton. This area, along with the territory between Sycamore and the eastern border of the canal, became primarily and increasingly home to new German immigrants. The area developed such a heavily German-dominated presence

The first steamboat traffic began in 1811. By the time this sketch was made in 1833, Cincinnati was becoming "the Queen City of the West," the hub of commerce west of the Appalachian Mountains. *From the collection of the Public Library of Cincinnati and Hamilton County.*

that the canal was nicknamed the "Rhine." Going over the canal into the German section was said to be going "over the Rhine," giving a name to the neighborhood that was growing so rapidly that contemporary observers said that streets and homes seemed to spring up almost overnight.

In 1848, a more serious revolutionary wave swept the German states and briefly threatened to establish national unity and democratic government. However, this attempt at revolution was also doomed for being more idealistic than strategic. Ground gained was quickly lost to overwhelming military strength. Authoritarian rule, execution of revolutionaries and mass exodus followed. The refugees who fled for political reasons became known as the "Forty-Eighters." It is unknown how many "Forty-Eighters" came to the United States because they arrived over a period of years in the late 1840s and '50s and because it is impossible to decipher political refugees from immigrants motivated purely by economic reasons, but the total number arriving in the United States is estimated between four and ten thousand. While there were few Forty-Eighters in overall numbers, they were influential leaders in the communities where they settled, including Over-the-Rhine.

These early waves of German immigrants helped bring more German immigrants. Letters home and accounts of American success in German publications brought friends, family and fellow countrymen. Strong early leadership in the German-American community and the German-heavy population of Over-the-Rhine made it a comfortable place for a new arrival, a community where it was unnecessary to speak English to find a job and conduct all the aspects of everyday life. Cincinnati was also a land of opportunity. Immigrants arriving in the 1850s and 1860s found a rapidly growing city with seemingly endless opportunities, many of them offered by the fellow German-Americans who preceded them. Although encouraged to learn English and the customs and traditions of their new country, German-Americans were also encouraged to retain their sense of independent identity. They waded into Americanism by reading tips from German-language papers and learning about the city through socialization in Over-the-Rhine saloons and through membership in German societies.

The city became home to a large number of the more than half a million Germans who flooded American shores just between 1852 and 1854 and the millions more who came in the following decades. New arrivals found more than a growing city with people who spoke their language. They found old world Gemütlichkeit (roughly translated as festive hospitality). The Germans were said to have brought the notion to America that it is a good thing to have a good time, and this spirit quickly began to permeate in the area of Cincinnati over the Rhine. Nationally and within Cincinnati, this was changing mores. When the first boats floated down the Miami and Erie Canal, drinking had become rare among the respectable middle class, and intoxication was scandalous. Two decades later, this had changed. In 1856, the Cincinnati Chamber of Commerce declared lager beer "a fashionable drink," and a few years later it observed that "Cincinnati had acquired the taste for 'Lager,' as a beverage, not only among the native German population, but all classes." The "Beer Gardens where this beverage is swallowed by old and young and in incredible quantities [had] become institutions of great magnitude." By the end of the Civil War, Over-the-Rhine's beer gardens were increasingly filled with the native born of all classes. Even devout Christians started to view total abstinence as old-fashioned. Lager beer became the drink of choice for young adults. It became so popular, in fact, that there was a decrease in per capita consumption of hard liquor even though per capita drinking remained steady. (Liquor consumption dropped 20 percent, and lager beer consumption increased 74 percent.) To the chagrin of temperance advocates, much of the middle-class stigma against drinking had disappeared and a much broader slice of America was enjoying a cold beer—but not everybody. In the mid-nineteenth century, the nation had become clearly divided between drinkers and abstainers. The division largely followed ethnic, religious and class lines, and it started to play an increasingly dominant role in politics.

AMERICA VERSUS
OVER-THE-RHINE

On February 3, 2010, former Colorado representative Tom Tancredo opened the first national conference of the Tea Party and drew national attention with the remark: "People who could not even spell the word 'vote' or say it in English put a committed socialist ideologue in the White House." Some Tea Party advocates expressed their unhappiness with the image these statements portrayed and noted that the Tea Party political movement had not previously emphasized anti-immigrant sentiments; but others view the anti-immigrant position as the logical extension of the rhetoric of Tea Party icons like Sarah Palin. When Palin was campaigning for vice president in 2008, she galvanized both support and opposition by calling "small towns" the "pro-America areas of this great nation"—the " *real* America."

The debate over what constitutes the "real America" is not new. In fact, it is as old as America itself. Who is or is not part of the "real America" has always contained a sense of cultural superiority over groups of people viewed to be of a lower moral caliber, and it usually involves ethnic and religious prejudices. "Real Americans" have long been the people who view a threat to their value system by major cultural shifts. The groups who threaten these values and what the values are themselves have changed over time, but the dynamic has remained eerily similar. Generations before "values voters" identified same-sex marriage as a threat to the nuclear family and the basic moral fiber of America, the temperance movement warned that legalized alcohol use was leading to the destruction of families and the nation's Christian morality.

The pre-Constitution Federalist Papers contained the following: "Providence has been pleased to give this one connected country to one united people—a people descended from the same ancestors, speaking the same language, professing the same religion, attached to the same principles of government, very similar in their manners and customs."

At the time, this was basically true. America was a pretty homogeneous place. Protestant Anglo-Saxons were the vast majority of the country. This began to change with immigration patterns in the 1830s and 1840s. As immigrants from Ireland and Germanic states started arriving on East Coast docks and making their way west, the question of the "real America" began. Did becoming an American mean becoming a citizen willing to defend the Constitution, or did it require assimilation—adopting both the language and customs of the early Anglo settlers?

The struggle over assimilation was not drawn strictly between immigrants and native-born Americans. It also played out within immigrant communities. In his 1854 German-American, urban crime novel, *Cincinnati, or Mysteries of the West,* author Emil Klauprecht (who was also a journalist and German-American historian) poses the different perspectives within the same household. The assimilation question is staged as the choices made by two brothers. Carl is "utterly Americanized." "His hair [is] cut and combed with extreme artificiality, no hair [is] not in its permitted place; his thin blond side-whiskers [lose] themselves in the snow white collar over his white cravat." Carl is "Americanized" in more than appearance. He has become humorless. His body is "without elasticity," and he lives for the "endless pursuit of business." Carl works tirelessly "without any recreation other than a fashionable concert or a Sunday sermon alongside his wife," an emasculating prude who objects to the use of the German language in her household. Carl wooed his wife by transcending his low-class German immigrant origins and becoming "a Yankee as bald and cold as any full-blooded native spawned in blessed Connecticut." Carl's son can "quote the price of bacon and flour with the precision of a commodity broker" but cannot speak a word of German.

By contrast, Carl's brother Wilhelm's "principal characteristics [are] the love of art and friendliness." He is a painter, and he is brooding. Reared in the "golden Rhineland, in that German paradise where every breath was a poetic joy," he cannot "simply shed his nature in a country which [surrounds] him with the limitless monotony of the mad hunt for money." The characters are a clear representation of the discussion about assimilation occurring within the German-American community of the 1850s. The "Thirtyers" were more inclined to assimilation and were politically more conservative. The "Forty-Eighters" were more liberal and tended to retain more of their ethnic identity. They were not rejecting America. They came here to embrace the idea of freedom and democracy but not a materialistic or puritanical value system. To many of these German-Americans there was no inconsistency between retaining their cultural heritage and also becoming true, patriotic Americans. In fact, Klauprecht turns the nativist assertion that the beer-swilling Germans were spreading immorality on its head, suggesting that the rejection of joy in favor of an endless quest for material wealth is the true root of immorality. As the spring election of 1855 neared, this struggle of ideologies about what it means to be a "real American" was about to play out in an election and an accompanying burst of urban warfare.

Cincinnati's German voters and the area known as Over-the-Rhine were becoming increasingly important in the 1850s and 1860s. Early German immigrants were relatively interspersed, and they also tended to be more politically conservative, mostly voting for the Whig Party. That changed when they started settling in Over-the-Rhine. Because native-born, English and other immigration continued at the same time that German immigration was increasing dramatically, the German population of the city remained relatively constant between 1840 and 1850—actually dropping from 28 percent to 26 percent due to the increase in total population—but German-American influence rose because of the concentration in Over-the-Rhine and adjacent voting blocs. The political bent of German-Americans also changed. The newer arrivals helped make the community overwhelmingly Democratic. In 1840, Germans were a minority in every ward. By 1850, they solidly controlled several wards, giving them council seats and power in mayoral elections. Two of these wards, the Eleventh and Twelfth, were above Liberty Street, an area that had been known as "the Northern Liberties" and had been outside of city limits until 1849.

On April 2, 1855, Cincinnatians went to the polls to vote to elect a mayor and a number of other municipal leaders. The mayoral candidates were a Democrat named James J. Faran and "Pap" Taylor, a member of the Cayenne Council Party. The Cayenne Council was the local manifestation of a national third-party movement. At the time, the Republican Party did not exist and the Whig Party was becoming irrelevant. That left a political vacuum that was filled by the American Party. Originally forming from a secret society known as the Order of the Star-Spangled Banner, and having different names at different locations and times, the American Party was most commonly known as the Know-Nothings because of its secretive origins. (Members would say that they knew nothing about the secret society if questioned publicly.) Know-Nothings were a nativist movement, a reaction to German and Irish immigration, and they were also anti-Catholic. They opposed the perceived threat that these groups posed to traditional American society.

Statewide, the Know-Nothings claimed 120,000 members in February 1855. Cincinnati had become the hotbed of the movement in the West both because of its large and rapidly increasing Irish and German populations and because of its position of local power. Although seemingly counterintuitive, Cincinnati's Germans had helped put the Know-Nothings in charge of municipal government in 1853 and in another round of elections in 1854. This happened because of the strategy of local Know-Nothings. They focused their campaign platform on opposition to slavery and cleaning up corrupt government, and they downplayed anti-immigrant messages. They were anti-Catholic, but this actually let them take advantage of a division between German Catholics and non-Catholic Germans who shared the Know-Nothing disdain of Catholics. Anti-Catholicism existed in the German-American community for a number of reasons. Some were broadly philosophical. Some were more tangible, local issues. Having fled failed attempts to establish less dictatorial governments in Germanic states, many of Cincinnati's German-American community were hostile to the Catholic Church for its role in helping monarchs crush rebellions across Europe. Some even feared the literal takeover of the American government by the Catholic Church. (Emil Klauprecht's novel referenced earlier is primarily about a plot by local Jesuits to use an old land claim to take over the city of Cincinnati.) There was also local conflict regarding the schools. Cincinnati's German-American community had been successful in getting German instruction incorporated into public school curriculum. Believing that this curriculum had a Protestant bent, the German Catholics sought matching funds for parochial education and occasionally opposed German instruction in public schools because they felt that it constituted unfair competition with their own private, Catholic schools.

In the previous years, Know-Nothings, under more innocuous names like the Cayenne Council, had succeeded at wooing non-Catholic German voters with their strategy of hushing anti-immigrant agendas in their ranks, focusing on issues that attracted Germans (like the abolition of slavery) and taking advantage of anti-Catholic sentiment within the German community. That worked for a while, but the movement could not keep its 1855 versions of Tom Tancredo fully contained. Anti-immigrant vitriol started busting out of the seams. Previously careful to maintain some distance from temperance advocates, this wall of separation also collapsed. German-American support waned quickly. The Cayenne Party entered the April 1855 elections solidly anti-immigrant, anti-Catholic and anti-alcohol. By making nativism and temperance the hallmarks of the movement, German-Americans were pushed to set aside religious or sectional squabbles and defend their culture and way of life: beer brought them together as a unified voting bloc.

The April 2 election was expected to bring change, and that change was poised to be delivered by the German-American wards in and around Over-the-Rhine. Every election produces winners and losers, but the Know-Nothings did not consider losing an option. Pap Taylor supporters were preparing to challenge the system of free elections in Cincinnati. Know-Nothingism seems to have been one of those periodically reoccurring movements in American politics that become defined by fringe members who are convinced, often fanatically and irrationally, that they are the defenders of nothing less than the soul of the nation; the protectors of decency, morality, social order and a Protestant-, Anglo-Saxon–based definition of what it means to be an American. To many local Know-Nothings, the April 2 election was more than an election. It was a war for control of the city, a war that was to be fought by the Americans against the foreigners, a war to be fought with the weapons of physical violence if the ballot was insufficient. And it was a war to be fought along the territorial boundaries of Cincinnati's "Rhine."

Over-the-Rhine was a distinctly German society in the mid-1800s. Its inhabitants looked different from other residents of the city. At a time when facial hair was frowned upon in polite society, many of the newly arrived Germans retained their thick beards and mustaches. They wore soft caps rather than the high, stiff ones popular with native-born Americans at the time. They spoke a different language, making German as common (or more so) on the streets of Over-the-Rhine as English. They had different customs and habits. Some of these were praised: their stereotypical cleanliness, organization and strong work ethic. Other traits brought much more scorn. Most notably, the Germans drank beer—a lot of it. During an

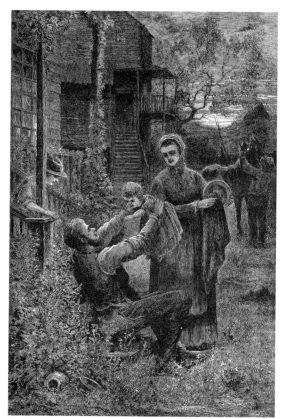

Above: Temperance proponents linked essentially all crime and poverty to alcohol consumption, arguing that moderate drinking was simply a gateway to destitution. Early temperance propaganda focused on "moral suasion," attempting to make drinkers abstinent for the good of their suffering families. *From the collection of the Public Library of Cincinnati and Hamilton County.*

Left: Temperance was promised to be the solution to almost all social ills. This nineteenth-century temperance propaganda also displays the cultural and social biases at work in the temperance and prohibition movements. Temperance, agrarian society and strong family bonds were all associated. Conversely, alcohol consumption was linked to immigrants, urbanization and crime. *From the collection of the Public Library of Cincinnati and Hamilton County.*

era when alcohol consumption had become generally unacceptable among "traditional" Anglo-American society, save for the occasional glass of wine among affluent friends, the German-Americans considered only drinking a gallon of beer at a social event to be a testament to moderation and often illustrated what a healthy alternative beer was to hard liquor by noting that it could be drunk all day long without feeling intoxication.

To the Know-Nothings, the Germans were not "real Americans." In fact, the area above the canal called Over-the-Rhine was contrasted with the area below the canal often referred to as "America." From the Know-Nothing perspective, residents of Over-the-Rhine were foreigners who refused to accept the traditional concept of American culture and therefore posed a threat to the city's very way of life. To the Know-Nothings, the April 2, 1855 election was nothing less than a decision between whether the city would be ruled by "Americans" or "foreign invaders."

Afraid of being outnumbered in an honest election, Know-Nothings went to Maysville, Kentucky, to recruit residents for a journey to Cincinnati. Early Monday morning, men from various local Know-Nothing lodges from several Kentucky towns began congregating at the public landing in Maysville, roughly sixty miles upriver from Cincinnati. They boarded the steamship *Daniel Boone*, and three hundred men, "armed to the teeth with revolvers and Bowie knives, and headed by prominent members of the Kentucky legislature," disembarked on the Cincinnati shore at about 10:00 a.m. on April 2, 1855, Election Day. According to the position of the Know-Nothings, these men were present to help keep the peace and ensure that the election was conducted fairly, without fraud perpetrated by immigrants or the party bosses who manipulated them. In fairness, Know-Nothing concerns about elections had a legitimate basis. By the time the Know-Nothing movement started to build steam in the 1840s, urban elections had become booze-laden carnivals of vote buying and fraud. For weeks leading up to an election, saloon patrons could drink free courtesy of political parties and their candidates. In addition, both voting laws and citizenship requirements were subject to manipulation. There was no unified, federalized system of obtaining citizenship. The process occurred through local courts. There was also no meaningful voter registration system. This made it easy for immigrants who had not yet become naturalized citizens to vote, and in the later era of machine politics it led to systems that directly exchanged naturalization court rulings for votes. There were legitimate problems with the democratic process caused by the fact that it was ill equipped to handle large waves of immigrants.

The Democratic-leaning *Daily Enquirer* took a different perspective on the Know-Nothing poll recruits, wryly noting that they had arrived to "protect the Cincinnati polls from the Irish." The paper observed that "armed as they were, they would be much more likely to excite than repress disturbance." The words were prophetic.

By noon, it was apparent to the Know-Nothings that they were losing the election. Violence began. In the Fifteenth Ward, the western side of downtown, a city councilman acting as a poll judge responded to some disagreement with a voter by brandishing and threatening him with a revolver. In the Fourteenth Ward, a Democrat "was very badly beaten with billies and other murderous weapons." In the largely Irish Fourth Ward, located on the eastern edge of the downtown basin, several Irishmen were attacked and beaten, and voters were chased away from the polls with Bowie knives. And in the heavily German Twelfth Ward, everything north of Liberty and east of Vine Street, "the butchers were particularly bellicose, and not only maltreated many of the peaceable disposed Germans but deterred a number from the polls."

The Know-Nothing attacks were aimed at both the Irish and the Germans, but there were a lot more Germans and the wards in and around Over-the-Rhine were critical to the outcome of the election. As a result, most of the violence started to focus on the German wards—mostly the Eleventh and Twelfth. Over-the-Rhine had been the site of an afternoon assault by Know-Nothings who "found themselves rather roughly handled." Entering the neighborhood to intimidate its inhabitants, a Covington resident named Pace received a trouncing instead. He and his nativist compatriots retreated to the sympathetic Fifteenth Ward to bring more recruits. When the Know-Nothings returned, they returned in force with the battle cry, "The Dutch must be whipped!" Throngs of Know-Nothings came from the wards that made up the affluent portions of what is now the southern part of the West End (ward Fifteen and Eight) and the central business district (the Fourteenth Ward) and made their way into Over-the-Rhine, "gathering in madness, numbers, and recklessness as they proceeded."

A brawl occurred around the F. Linck Brewery on McMicken Avenue (then called Hamilton), a little west of Walnut Street. Escalating the general intimidation and bullying, a Know-Nothing man attacked and stabbed the brewery foreman, a German named George Reeder. He clung to life but succumbed and passed away several days later. Reeder had fought back. Original reports indicated that he wrestled the knife from his assassin, a Covington resident named Lee Pettit, and killed him instantly.[1] As Reeder lay bleeding, groups of "loafers and Know-Nothing rowdies, faces inflamed with whiskey, streamed on foot, on horseback and in buggies towards Hamilton Road, yelling like savages 'Hurrah for Pap Taylor!'"

As these events unfolded, a group of Germans had been holding a celebration of Thomas Jefferson's birthday on Jackson Hill,[2] periodically shooting off a cannon as part of the ceremonies. The mob of Know-Nothings misinterpreted the cannon fire as a victory celebration for the election. A couple hundred Know-Nothings stormed the unsuspecting celebrants. They trampled through the peaceful crowd and took the cannon by force. Although many of the Germans were armed, the Know-Nothings experienced very little resistance from the bewildered crowd. At roughly 6:00 p.m. on election eve, the mob hauled the cannon down the hill to a position across from the Eleventh Ward polling location. They planned on firing it at the polls. Active mayor Snellbaker rode up to the group on horseback and persuaded the mob to march the cannon down to the river and fire it in a safe manner. That prevented the cannon from being shot at the polling location, but the Know-Nothings decided to take the Eleventh Ward ballot box on their way out of Over-the-Rhine.

Mayor Snellbaker again tried to intervene, but this time less successfully: "He received a blow in the side from a brick-bat, which prostrated him; his coat was torn in shreds from his back, and he was considerably injured." A current city councilman named Dale also attempted to protect the ballot box but was knocked down in front of the door and beaten with a table leg. The mob then seized the ballot box and destroyed the ballots—eliminating an estimated nine hundred Democratic votes—and proceeded on their march with the cannon in tow.

They made their way to the Thirteenth Ward poll (Pendleton) with the intent of destroying the ballots there as well. The plan was to start firing

---

1. Sources differ significantly on this story. The foreman's name may have been Roder, and his assailant may have been a Dr. Brown from Cincinnati. Dr. Brown later made a public declaration that he was alive and well. It is unclear whether he was alive because Reeder (or Roder) did not, in fact, kill his assassin or because Pettit from Covington, not Brown from Cincinnati, was the killer.

2. Jackson Hill does not appear on maps of the time. It was most likely the area now know as Jackson Hill Park, just above Mulberry Street, east of Vine Street.

the cannon at the polling location and then destroy the ballots after most of the resistance had been driven away (or killed). Likely due to advance warning, the polling location had been closed "minutes before" and the votes were secured. The Know-Nothings moved the cannon to the corner of the street, and "notwithstanding men, women and children [who in] great alarm and consternation were fleeing in every direction," the mob began firing various projectiles from the cannon indiscriminately down Sycamore Street. One of these blasts sent a large rock smashing into the skull of a "poor laborer" immigrant who was unlucky enough to be driving a cart at the wrong place and time. He died from the wound two days later. The mob then moved through the streets of the city committing various acts of violence and destruction.

Polling locations friendly to the Cayenne Council remained peaceful, suffering no similar repercussions from Democratic or immigrant groups. The only acts or threats of violence in these locations seem to have come from the Cayenne themselves. Particularly in the early stages of violence, most of the German community appears to have responded to threats and attacks with what might be called civil obedience: they "practiced the virtue of patience" and tried to maintain order. However, as mob violence escalated, this strategy required modification. There were no counterattacks on Cayenne-favored polls, but self-defense became more aggressive.

A subsequent assault on the Irish Fourth Ward didn't turn out as planned. Ready with shotguns and stones, the Irish Americans beat down the Know-Nothing hordes, seized the cannon and returned it to the Germans; but issues surrounding the cannon would not die. It seems to have attained symbolic significance that far exceeded its actual usefulness in deciding a municipal election. On the following day, it would reappear as the ridiculous justification for armed urban warfare.

On April 3, the morning edition of the *Daily Enquirer* announced that the vote count by 3:00 a.m. was sufficient to declare victory for the entire Democratic slate "notwithstanding the rape of the ballot box in the Eleventh Ward." The announcement of a "glorious Democratic victory" was premature. Two more days of violence were still in store. Keen to the fact that they were losing the election, Know-Nothing poll judges in the Twelfth Ward (Over-the-Rhine and the German West End, north of Liberty and west of Vine Street) concluded that there were 52 more votes cast than there were registered voters. While votes were still being counted in a firehouse, a mob of about four hundred Know-Nothings forced its way inside, "grabbed the ballots, poll books, and voter lists and tossed them into the fireplace." This resulted in the destruction of the Twelfth Ward ballots, making the total destroyed votes reach 1,300. Before the Twelfth Ward ballots were destroyed, the entire Democratic slate was reportedly winning by 626 votes citywide. The allegation of over-counts was later disproven as a scriber's error, and the *Daily Enquirer* astutely questioned why the response to alleged vote fraud was the destruction of the evidence of the alleged crime. Nevertheless, this baseless allegation of immigrant vote packing became the rallying cry that brought the full attention of the Know-Nothings on the heavily German Eleventh and Twelfth Wards.

Although the Germans' ceremonial cannon had only been used to perpetrate one act of violence, and on that occasion by the Know-Nothings themselves, it became the justification for war on "the Rhine." Red leaflets were scattered throughout the "American" parts of the city calling all the like-minded to a meeting at the Fifth Street Market. Plans for further Know-Nothing attacks were made. Pap Taylor, the mayoral candidate himself, is reported to have traveled around to different locations advising armies of nativists that the bell at Mechanic's Hall (at the corner of Sixth and Vine) would ring to rally forces together if any of the "Americans" got into trouble in foreign wards. Armed and organized, the Know-Nothings established an encampment on the Vine Street bridge over the canal and demanded that the Germans surrender their cannon.

Reference to police presence during these days of riot is mysteriously sparse, particularly in light of police reaction to previous disturbances within the German community. Two years before, a group of Protestant German-Americans organized to protest the visit of Catholic Archbishop Bedini. At least according to popular belief, papal nuncio Archbishop Gaetano Bedini had been responsible for the massacre of Italian revolutionaries in Bologna. The German-language press suggested that the "Butcher of Bologna" deserved summary justice while in Cincinnati, and anti-Catholic rhetoric reigned in the German-American community. A meeting was held in Freemen's Hall on December 21, 1853, and a group of between eight hundred and one thousand protestors put together a straw man in a bishop's robe, hung it from a gallows and began marching down Vine Street, leaving Over-the-Rhine and headed to the Catholic cathedral on Plum Street. The plan was to burn Bedini's straw effigy in front of the church on Christmas Eve.

The protest had violent undertones, but it was being conducted in an orderly and peaceful manner when all seventy-five members of Cincinnati's police force flanked its sides. Without ordering the crowd to disperse or making any attempt to reach a peaceful resolution, the police began shooting at the crowd, firing shotguns indiscriminately into the group without regard for the screams of women and children within it. They pounced upon people trying to flee, beat them with lead slings and dragged them to the station—including several completely innocent bystanders. At least one young man was murdered by police bullets, and dozens received beatings.

As vicious, murderous and unconstitutional as the police behavior was, it demonstrates clear precedence in responding to potential mob violence. Although there seems to have been little resistance, many of the protestors were carrying revolvers and swords, and they outnumbered the police at least ten to one. While the reaction to the 1853 protest was wrong, it was also effective. By contrast, the police appear to have taken an essentially passive role as mobs of thugs destroyed ballots, assaulted the mayor, roamed through the streets beating and stabbing people and fired off a cannon down a crowded city street. Some sources suggest that this was intentional, that the same police force quick to butcher a peaceful procession of protestors was equally willing to stand by and let the same ethnic group be viciously attacked. It is also possible that the mobs were of such size and so heavily armed that the relatively inexperienced police force was simply unequipped for such a large-scale problem, but there never appears to have been any more than five hundred rioters at one place and time—about half the number who were dispersed in the 1853 protest. Whatever the reason, the Cincinnati police appear to have been of very little use during the 1855 election riot "and carried out their duties only at the pleasure of the mob." Given their behavior two years earlier, maybe that was actually the best scenario that the city's immigrants could hope for.

The county sheriff did play a role in attempts to negotiate peace. Although the German-Americans refused to deal directly with Know-Nothing leaders, they agreed to negotiate peace terms through the sheriff. A deal was reached: if the Germans surrendered the cannon to the protective custody of the sheriff, the Know-Nothings would stand down. The Germans agreed to place the cannon barrel in the sheriff's possession. It was loaded onto a wagon, minus its carriage (the rolling stand used to fire it), and led over the canal.

The plan was to take the cannon and its carriage to the armory for safekeeping. This did not satisfy the nativist mobs, who called it a trick. The sheriff was attacked, and the cannon was seized by the Know-Nothings at Fourth and Broadway. It was dragged back up to the corner of Walnut and Canal with the mob demanding the rolling stand. One of the German-American leaders responded to the demands by saying that they would give up the carriage "to legal authority, but not to a mob." The sheriff regained control of the situation, and the carriage was surrendered as well, with the hope that handing over the gun that had become such an unlikely centerpiece of the conflict would end the violence.

Over-the-Rhine's forays into peace were made in vain. Despite earlier assurances, possession of the cannon did nothing to pacify the Know-Nothing army. They demanded that all small arms and ammunition also be surrendered to the "Americans" and taken from the hands of the foreign-born. "The Germans had no confidence in the promises of men who had so recently given evidence of their utter disregard of law, order, and honesty, and preferred holding on to their arms, and, if need be, dying [in battle]."

On day two of the violence, a headline in the morning *Daily Enquirer* read, "A City in Arms: Mob Law Triumphant." Rumor and speculation ran rampant through the city, particularly in Over-the-Rhine. The first American Turner Society was founded in Over-the-Rhine in 1848. Dedicated to keeping unity within the German-American community and promoting the German-American role in American democracy, the society served a critical role in helping newly arrived German immigrants acclimate to the city and promoting German culture. It was also integral in pushing awareness of physical fitness and was primarily responsible for making physical education part of public school curriculum. Turnhalle, or Central Turner Hall, was on Walnut Street. It was the Turner society's home and also served other German societies. Freemen's Hall on the corner of Mercer and Vine was another of Over-the-Rhine's German societies with a physically substantial headquarters. The society's primary mission was the abolition of slavery and the promotion of democracy. Militancy was not an aspect of either society, but for several days in April 1855, their philanthropic goals became a secondary concern to literal survival. Both the Central Turner Hall and Freemen's Hall became armed fortresses.

Throughout the buildings, "muskets, bristling with bayonets were piled in the rooms." Outside, the stores of Over-the-Rhine were closed, and "men

During the 1855 election violence, Central Turner Hall was transformed from a center of German societies and cultural life to an armed encampment, one of two stockpiles for weapons and ammunition during the three days of violence. (Both Central Turner Hall, 1411 Walnut Street, and Freemens' Hall, corner of Mercer and Vine, have been demolished.) *From the collection of the Public Library of Cincinnati and Hamilton County.*

paraded the streets with stern features, and armed to the teeth." Caught essentially unaware and unprepared for the assaults on Election Day, the German-American residents of Over-the-Rhine prepared to defend their homes and their families and, if necessary, to fight to the death to repel an invasion by the "Americans." The canal jokingly nicknamed "the Rhine" became a line of actual military demarcation between warring nationalities. Rumors began to spread that a large-scale attack was planned on Over-the-Rhine. A neighborhood spokesman said, "We have been assaulted and abused…they have assaulted our dearest privileges as citizens by their outrage upon our ballot-boxes, and now we are threatened with an attack upon our homes…They would murder us in cold blood, and we would be unworthy the privileges we enjoy as American citizens were we to quietly submit to further indignity." Over-the-Rhine residents, many of whom were veterans of wars abroad, barricaded and fortified the bridges over the canal.

Violence escalated. At roughly 5:00 p.m. on Tuesday, April 3, the crowd in control of the Vine Street bridge started shouting "Hurrah for Pap Taylor!" This jubilant support for the Know-Nothing mayoral candidate sparked a

Know-Nothing proponents of mayoral candidate Pap Taylor encamped on the Vine Street bridge over the canal and conducted armed raids into Over-the-Rhine during the 1855 election riots. This photo was taken decades later, from roughly the vantage point of the sidewalk beside the Kroger building. The buildings on the northeast corner were demolished long ago, and the site now houses the aesthetically challenged Gateway building. The building containing the wine bar on the northwest corner has also been demolished, but the neighboring property that now displays the large mural of Jim Tarbell can be discerned. *Courtesy of the Cincinnati Historical Society Library, Cincinnati Museum Center.*

German move from defense to offense. German-Americans marched from their fortified positions in Over-the-Rhine and engaged the Know-Nothings in a gun battle. The Germans drove the battalion of bigots from the Vine Street bridge. There were "a number of firearms being discharged, and numberless missiles hurled," and "the danger at one time was imminent," but no serious injury was reported from this skirmish.

Raids were conducted into Over-the-Rhine throughout the day. Plans were laid to seize Freemen and Turner Halls. At 10:00 p.m., a band of Know-Nothings began marching from the affluent central financial and business district to Freemen's Hall. They marched in military manner with a drum and fifer in the lead. They somehow made it across one of the fortified bridges, or maybe they took a more circuitous route. Expecting little resistance, they stood on the west side of Vine Street and began loading their muskets for an assault on the hall. Rather than the turkey shoot that they were expecting, the German citizens of Over-the-Rhine hit them with a volley of bullets "from all sides." Those who could "fled like rabbits" to their encampment on the south side of the Vine Street bridge; but some were unable to retreat. An Indiana Know-Nothing who was in town for the election violence was shot in the head and fell dead on the spot. Two other men appeared to be fatally wounded, one with a bullet through the throat and the other receiving a lead ball in the stomach. Numerous other invaders were severely wounded.

Know-Nothings held a large public meeting at Mechanic's Hall. Cincinnatians were living "terror-stricken in fear of what the next hour would bring." The governor of Ohio, who was in Baltimore on business, sent the attorney general to Cincinnati by train, granting him authority to call out militia and guardsmen if necessary. Random attacks on immigrants were occurring throughout the city. A German-American simply walking down the street in the central business district was jumped and beaten with shouts of ethnic epithets. A "gang of rowdies, armed with every variety of weapons," entered a saloon on Front Street. After having a few drinks, they refused to pay. When the German owner asked them to leave, "they beat him and smashed up his shop." They left and attacked three more Germans in the street, mortally stabbing one of them.

There is no deeply meaningful, satisfying reason for why the battle Over-the-Rhine concluded. Nativist sentiments were not quelled. No great act of diplomacy occurred. Three days and nights of ethnic urban warfare came to an end because it started to rain. On "Wednesday night, at a time when riot and disorganization had seemed to have arrived at the highest pitch, and sober peaceable men were trembling under the influence of fearful anticipation of the night of horror, the clouds poured down their welcome torrent, acting upon the occasion as oil upon the angry waves of popular commotion." It all stopped suddenly just as if three days and nights of armed conflict, of election riots that seemed to threaten the future of democracy in Cincinnati, had all been a little league game. The war ended because day four "was an exceedingly unpleasant day, abounding in mud, slush, and rain." In the immediate days following, "the channel of communication to our brethren over the Rhine was again open…business in that part of the city was once more resumed, and peace and good will had effectively banished the elements of discord and confusion."

Although they proceeded in a far less violent manner, election disputes continued. Despite attempts of the members of the Cayenne Party to distance themselves from both the Know-Nothings and the days of mob violence and editorial assurances that they would, in honor and good faith, never attempt to take unfair advantage of any election irregularities like the destruction of ballot boxes, Pap Taylor declared himself victorious. On the day the rain came, the Cayenne Party went to the clerk of courts to certify the election in favor of their slate of candidates. The clerk refused certification. After several days of heated but nonviolent political wrangling, votes in the Eleventh and Twelfth Wards were re-created by logbooks. On the following Monday, Taylor's opponent, James J. Faran, was officially declared the mayor of the city of Cincinnati. The Eleventh and Twelfth Ward votes put him over the top, along with a number of other Democratic candidates that would have otherwise lost the election.

In Cincinnati, democracy had prevailed and a hard rain had restored peace, but the incidents in Over-the-Rhine were repeated in other cities. Columbus's German-American community was also the site of ethnic bloodletting. In Cleveland, Know-Nothings praised the large African American turnout for their candidates, pontificating that "[t]he colored people are natives, and much better citizens than the hordes of Catholic Irish who are yearly floating to our shores." But the worst outbreak of Know-Nothing violence in the Midwest seems to have been in Louisville, Kentucky. It was the next municipal election occurring in the region after Cincinnati's, and the city had a large German-American population (estimated before the election at roughly eighteen thousand). During the days of bloodshed in Cincinnati, the *Daily Enquirer* expressed various well wishes to the inhabitants of Louisville. The paper expressed the hope that the people of the city would learn from the violence in Cincinnati and prevent a similar catastrophe in their own town, but events took a very different turn. The violence in Louisville was far worse.

The amount of blood spilled in Louisville occurred, in part, due to gambling. Prior to the election, a motley collection of Know-Nothing thugs and politically indifferent professional gamblers had wagered large sums on Louisville election results. With motivations ranging from purely financial to ideologically xenophobic, hordes of violent thugs descended on Louisville to help ensure Know-Nothing victories. If the immigrant populations of Louisville failed to learn from Cincinnati, the Know-Nothings learned plenty. There was less need to destroy ballots because Know-Nothings were more efficient at preventing votes from being cast. Mobs were in control of all the polls by 10:00 a.m., threatening off all Germans and Irish with stones and knives. The first skirmish occurred at 11:00 a.m. when German and Irish immigrants administered a sound beating to "American" thugs. This enraged the Know-Nothings, and they began roaming the city looking for revenge on random immigrants. A German man who was sitting on his porch enjoying a beer and a pipe had a mob descend upon his home. "All his possessions, for which he had worked the best years of his life, were destroyed and the life of his family threatened." A German-owned saloon was smashed to pieces. A German-owned grocery was looted and vandalized. And the mobs increased in firepower and viciousness. A German brewery was burned to the ground and workers beaten. A factory, a barrel repair shop, bakeries, groceries, homes and other German-American-owned buildings were vandalized or burned down. "Unfortunate women, children in their arms...fled in all directions." Their men "plead for mercy from the mob, over which waved the Stars and Stripes." Gangs chased down random German and Irish immigrants and murdered them in the streets, shooting some and beating others to death.

As Election Day in Louisville plodded bloodily along toward evening, it became increasingly common to burn the homes and tenements occupied by German-American and Irish-American families. German-American historian Emil Klauprecht described the terror:

> *The unfortunate ones who tried to escape the flames met death in other forms. As soon as one would appear on the doorstep, he would be shot down. Many were dragged away seriously wounded; others, bloodied and maimed, crawled back into the flaming houses to avoid falling into the hands of the savages. It was impossible to flee from the houses without being killed. It is impossible to tell how many of these unfortunate people were trapped in their homes and burned alive.*

Immediately following the election violence in Louisville, at least one hundred German-American families packed up their remaining belongings and moved, many to friendlier territory in Wisconsin. There was no similar exodus from Cincinnati, and as bad as the violence was in Over-the-Rhine, it cannot be compared to the horrific carnage in Louisville. In fact, with the exception of an unlucky few who were caught outnumbered and unaware in the central business district—the "poor laborer" shot by the cannon, a German-American who accidentally shot himself and the foreman of the F. Linck Brewery who was attacked early in the violence—most of the body count appears to have been accumulated by the Know-Nothings at the hands of able German defenders. Cincinnati's "Rhine" provided a strategic military advantage that did not exist in Louisville, and Over-the-Rhine seems to have been better equipped. Although taken initially off guard, the leadership in Over-the-Rhine turned the neighborhood into a defensible encampment in a matter of hours, erecting barricades and turning two strategically close but separate halls into armories and safe zones. The squabbles among different German-American organizations would continue, particularly over the Catholic Church's role in German language instruction, but the primary effect of the Know-Nothing attacks was to bring the German-Americans together in a more cohesive and organized manner than before. Ironically, an attack on a community motivated largely by their refusal to assimilate strengthened their ethnic loyalty.

There are other versions of the events surrounding the 1855 election. Some local papers essentially ignored it. Some played up the allegations of vote fraud. The *New York Herald* relayed the events to the nation with a decidedly anti-German bent: "A savage riot occurred at the election in Cincinnati yesterday, between the foreigners and Americans. The ballot boxes were, of course, destroyed at the outset; and whether the Know Nothings or the 'Sag-Night' party elected their candidate could not be ascertained…The Dutch paraded with a loaded cannon, bidding defiance to their adversaries."

While there are always at least two sides to every story, the German-American version of this one simply makes more sense. Allegations of vote packing seem ridiculous based on the presumably objective fact that only ninety-six more people voted in the spring election in 1855 than voted in the fall of 1854 and that Know-Nothing candidates were already trending down. Attempts to characterize the Germans as aggressors also seem ridiculous since the Know-Nothings imported hundreds of armed flunkies and all of the violence centered on attacks on the immigrant polls. And local officials seem to have agreed by acknowledging fraud and refusing to certify Cayenne election results minus Over-the-Rhine votes.

By the week following the April 2, 1855 election, the German-Americans and Irish-Americans had won. They had successfully defended their homes, their families, their lives and their right to participate in local politics and had even won an election. For a moment, for some, the question of what it meant to be a "real American" had been answered. More tangibly, Over-the-Rhine had established itself as a critical source of political power in Cincinnati, a power that would even extend to statewide elections in years to follow. Unlike Irish-Americans who were overwhelmingly Catholic and overwhelmingly, consistently Democratic, the German-Americans were less predictable. They valued ethnic loyalty over party loyalty. When presented with the option to do so, they voted more for their interests than for a party. For roughly the next sixty years, Over-the-Rhine would continue to be critical in winning city elections. Fulfilling the fears of Know-Nothings, it would also help give rise to an era of machine politics. Fulfilling the fears of the temperance wing of the Know-Nothing movement, Over-the-Rhine would most frequently flex its muscle when it came to the issue that became known as "personal liberty." Over-the-Rhine's German-Americans could be divided in a number of ways, and the community had internal factions that disagreed on just about everything, but the most consistent way to bring them together as a mobilized force was to threaten their beer.

The election of 1855 marked the end of power for the Cayenne Party locally, and the national American Reform Party and Know-Nothingism would also soon disappear. The Know-Nothing movement was ultimately brought to an end by the start of the Civil War and the emergence of the Republican Party. Two-party rule reemerged and became the standard of American politics. Nativism didn't disappear. It emerged in the two parties in the form of different issues. The nature of the battle lines remained the same.

On April 6, 1855, just one day after a torrential rain stopped the violence, the *Daily Enquirer* printed a small story that read in its entirety: "The Main Law Passed—After a strong but steadily-resisted effort to kill the Prohibition Law in the Senate, by annoying and injurious amendments, the vote was taken last evening and the bill passed—yeas 21, nays 11."

The Main Law was the nation's first statewide prohibition law. It would not be the last. In roughly the next three-quarters of a century, issues surrounding immigration, ethnicity, race relations, crime and the battle between the inhabitants of America's cities versus those of "real America" would increasingly focus on one issue. While the German-American community called the issue "personal liberty," a primarily native-born, Protestant, Anglo-Saxon army of religious crusaders was already calling it "prohibition." Regardless of what you called it, continuing prohibition efforts and the post–Civil War spike in the popularity of German lager beer and Over-the-Rhine's beer gardens represented much more than just a fight over alcohol. Before gay marriage, abortion rights, civil rights or the Vietnam War, beer became the focal point of a much broader social debate.

THE GOLDEN AGE
OF GOLDEN BEER

Beer has always been part of our national culture. Colonial America was full of home-brew recipes with varying ingredients and fermentation periods as short as a day. There seems to have been several problems with early beer as a commodity, but the largest might have been the fact that a lot of it—maybe most of it—wasn't very good. Beer fermented in a day may work out nicely if you're in prison or concerned that the local water supply will give you dysentery, but you wouldn't drink it if you had a better choice. Beer as we know it today is a relatively modern delicacy that was first crafted around the mid-1800s. Before that, Cincinnatians did have beer options, but a thirsty Cincinnatian was more likely to drink whiskey or wine.

In fact, the Ohio River Valley was the early nineteenth-century version of wine country. Cincinnati's first café, given the austere name of Pegasus and the Fallen Poet, was opened by a Frenchman in 1793. He cultivated grapes in a lot next to the café and established the Ohio Valley's first vineyard. It would not be alone in the region for long. Vevay, Indiana, about sixty miles downstream from Cincinnati, was producing 2,400 gallons of wine a year as early as 1810. Production had more than doubled by 1817. Vevay's vintners predicted that their output, quality and access to Cincinnati as a shipping port would soon eliminate America's need to import European wine. While this prediction didn't come true, the area's vintners had reason for optimism. By 1848, there were 743 acres of vineyard within a twenty-mile radius of Cincinnati

Even Cincinnati's early Germans had a closer connection to wine than beer. Nicholas Longworth was Cincinnati's most noted vintner, covering much of the hills overlooking the city with grapevines. Longworth was not German, but the majority of his vineyard employees were. By the late 1840s, German immigrants were supplying the majority of vineyard workers, and they were producing respected wine. During a trip to Cincinnati, former president Martin Van Buren compared local wine to the best wines that he had tasted in Europe, and Cincinnati's famed Catawba won a medal in an 1850 London competition.

The beer did not fare so well. Local historian Robert J. Wimberg has found evidence of a commercial brewery on Cincinnati's waterfront as early as 1806 but concedes that very little is known about this alleged first brewery. It is probably safe to assume that the beer was not well received and that the operation went out of business in short order, because nineteenth-century historians overlook its existence entirely. The title of first commercial Cincinnati brewery is more commonly given to an Englishman named Embree. In January 1812, Embree started producing "Draught Beer…Porter and Ale, manufactured in the best Philadelphia manner." It must have been a welcome development to be able to order a beer in a Cincinnati tavern, but the drinker's ethnicity may have determined whether Embree was getting it right. In 1816, a traveler with the Anglo name of David Thomas called Embree's brewery one of the "most respectable of the manufacturing establishments" in Cincinnati and declared the beer "excellent." Nineteenth-century historian Emil Klauprecht recorded the less-favorable German perspective. He described Embree's beer as being of "poor quality." Nor did Klauprecht characterize beer made at the time by people that he considered fellow countrymen with much higher regard: "Not even the construction of the first German brewery by Billiod and Jonte could avert this national calamity," noting that the "beer brewed at that time would not stay fresh in the summer." (Billiod and Jonte were actually French Alsatians.) Beer remained a minor factor in Cincinnati's early alcoholic beverage industry during the 1820s. Embree went out of business in 1825, leaving just two other breweries. One was operated by another Englishman and one by an Irishman named O'Reilly.

The first German-owned brewery is reported to have been a small operation started in Over-the-Rhine in 1829, at what is roughly the corner of McMicken Avenue and the top of Elm Street. Wimberg writes that "there are few records" of this first Cincinnati German brewer named Schmelzer, and, in fact, no one with this name is listed in the 1829 city directory, nor is there any reference to a brewery at this location. A lack of corroborating evidence may be attributable to the brewery's size and where it was located. The brewery was described as nothing more than a "little old house," and in 1829, the city limits stopped at Liberty Street, blocks south of Schmelzer's brewery. What is indisputable is that the site eventually became home to the Jackson Brewery in the 1850s.

If Schmelzer existed, he was an anomaly. Cincinnati's brewing industry started to grow slowly, and almost entirely without Germans. By the 1840s, breweries were a significant aspect of Cincinnati's manufacturing economy. The popularity of beer was likely aided by the state of the water. Even though the city had built its first waterworks in 1819, city water was not an attractive option. In 1845, the *Cincinnati Commercial* wrote that the state of the city's reservoir was deplorable. It had muddy water flowing straight into it, dead animals floating on the surface and an industrial operation spewing poisonous byproducts just twenty feet away. Whether or not it satisfied a discerning German palate, beer was safer than water. There were at least eight breweries in operation during the '40s, and all were distinctly non-German. With the exception of Irish O'Reilly, all were owned by ethnically English or Frenchmen, and they tended to employ fellow countrymen. The Germans stuck to winemaking, baking and other professions, but changes were happening in Germanic states that were about to change Cincinnati's drink of choice.

While there were a number of failed revolutionary and reform movements in Germanic states in the 1830s and 1840s, one German revolution succeeded spectacularly and changed the world: the lager revolution. For the first few thousand years of beer's history, it was made with yeast strains that ferment at the top of the vat. Lager beer used yeast strains that create a bottom-fermented brew. Unlike its predecessors, it also required fermentation at about forty degrees Fahrenheit. After it was made, it would also spoil if it wasn't kept chilled. Some of the best modern beers are porters and ales, and some early beers of these varieties may have been very good, but as a general rule the beer made prior to lager seems to have been inferior to the beer made after the introduction of lager yeast. This seems to have occurred for several related reasons. First, lager was more difficult to make and required a longer fermentation period than was typical of earlier beers. It also needed to be kept cool during fermentation. Making lager beer was more complicated than making early ales, porters and what was called

The Banner Brewery at the northeast corner of Walnut and Canal (now Central Parkway) was a good example of regal brewing architecture. Its copula and the building farthest to the east have elements in common with the very ornate Sohn Brewery on McMicken. Bought by a consortium of saloon owners and labor leaders who were angry with the brewing industry, the brewery became the Cincinnati Consumers' Brewing Company in its final year. This photo was taken after a fire in 1909. It was never reopened and was razed for the construction of the Ohio College of Applied Science (now the Emery Building) in 1911. *Courtesy of the Cincinnati Historical Society Library, Cincinnati Museum Center.*

"common beer." It took more time and effort and required finding solutions to the challenge of keeping beer cool prior to artificial refrigeration, but it was worth it because it made a much better beer. At the advent of lager beer production in Germany in the 1830s, the Industrial Revolution was already transforming Europe and North America and changing the way that virtually all products were made. The discovery of lager corresponded with these broader social changes and helped drive a fundamental change in the nature of commercial beer production.

In his history of Cincinnati brewing, *Over the Barrel*, Timothy J. Holian chronicles the mysterious origins of lager beer in both Germany and the United States. "The most common explanation holds that Gabriel Sedlmayr II of Munich and Anton Dreher of Vienna first successfully introduced the new yeast in southern Europe in the 1830s," but Holian notes an intriguing theory. In the 1820s and 1830s, Sedlmayr befriended an Austrian brewer, and the pair traveled around England visiting breweries and doing what might politely be referred to as learning brewing techniques. The more blunt description of their technique is theft. In later years, "the two recalled their propensity for stealing wort and yeast samples for their own use," leaving the intriguing possibility that the key ingredient to German lager beer may have been stolen from England.

The introduction of lager beer in America is equally mysterious, and Cincinnati may play a leading role in the story. Yeast are living microorganisms. There are about 1,500 known species of yeast and thousands more believed to exist. Different species live, thrive or die in different conditions. Some prefer subfreezing temperatures. Some thrive at over one hundred degrees Fahrenheit. The yeast typically used to make ales and porters thrive in higher temperatures, whereas lager yeast needs to stay cool. That posed a challenge in transporting the yeast from Europe to the United States when the journey took weeks and ice storage or traveling in winter would have been the only methods of refrigeration. Once on American soil, transporting the yeast by horse or riverboats would have presented the same challenge. It makes sense that the first production would have occurred around the East Coast, and the most commonly accepted history traces the first American lager production to a small brewery in Philadelphia. However, Timothy Holian writes:

> *Several accounts have been offered of pioneer lager brewers in Cincinnati, but most suffer from serious flaws in historical accuracy—not to mention a lack of evidence—and as a result may be discounted. Karl Ludwig Fleischmann was credited with the introduction of lager beer in the city as early as 1834. According to a later report, Fleischmann brewed just enough lager to supply customers at his Main Street saloon. The brew reputedly met with great success, and Fleischmann was inspired to construct a lager beer cellar nearby, at the corner of Main and Abigail (later Twelfth) Streets, one year later. But a lack of evidence to support the claim—including the fact that no proof exists of commercial lager production in Europe before the Fleischmann venture—and an equally notable scarcity of information on how the requisite strain of lager yeast got to Cincinnati, make it difficult to accept the story.*

Holian's logic is sound, and the account of Fleischmann's 1834 lager beer was a reminiscence written decades after the fact, but "coincidences" and some unknowns create a possible mystery. Fleischmann does not appear in the 1834 city directory. However, the city directories were effectively recording information from the previous year, and the directory for 1835 is missing from every library or historical collection in the city.[3] Fleischmann was supposed to have built the brewery to serve his saloon on Main Street. The city directory lists a "Lewis C. Flushman" residing at roughly where the saloon was supposed to be on Main and lists his occupation as brewer. It also lists a Bavarian Brewery owned by a "Flashman" at the location of the illusive Fleischmann Brewery. Anglo Cincinnatians frequently had difficulty with foreign names, and they were often "Americanized." Ludwig often became Louis; Karl could be spelled Carl. Therefore, it seems plausible that Karl Ludwig Fleischmann and Louis C. Flushman and Flashman were all the same person. If so, it proves that Fleischmann's brewery existed by at least 1835—still before the first accepted account of lager production in 1840 Philadelphia. None of these names appears in the 1834 directory, suggesting that Fleischmann came to Cincinnati with enough money and knowledge to immediately obtain property and start brewing.

Early breweries came and went, but why the Fleischmann brewery closed and what happened to Fleischmann raise questions. The business failure is not attributable to unpopularity. Fleischmann had to sell because he got overextended building his "lager brewery." He then moved to Washington, D.C., to work in the patent office. After Fleischmann's departure, the "lager brewery" was bought by Conrad Muentzenberger and Francis Fortmann, who operated Fortaman's Bavarian Brewery, which appears to be the historically accepted origin of lager beer in Cincinnati. Maybe the 1880 reminiscence of Fleischmann's lager beer got the location correct but inaccurately recalled the ownership or year. Maybe that explains the coincidence between the same location being both the *disputed* first Cincinnati brewery to make lager in 1834 and the *accepted* first brewery to make it by 1846. Maybe there is nothing particularly intriguing about Fleischmann's business failure, but why did a successful saloon owner and small brewer drive himself into financial collapse building a brewery, and did the building contain lagering tunnels?

3. The 1835 directory is missing from the Hamilton County Public Library, the Cincinnati Museum Center, the Mercantile Library and the University of Cincinnati's libraries. Neither the Kenton County Library nor Campbell County Library has a copy, nor does Xavier University.

Prior to the introduction of lager yeast, beer could be brewed essentially anywhere. Lagering tunnels could have been used for beer storage but would not have been necessary for the beer's production. Were they added underneath the existing brewery that Fleischmann built sometime before the same facility was indisputably producing lager beer a few years later, or did Fleischmann run out of money digging subbasements and building the first facility for lager beer production in the United States? Is it purely coincidental that the man who was reported to be making lager at a time when it was essentially unknown even in Germany left his "lager brewery" in Cincinnati and went to D.C. to work in the patent office? Probably, but there is an unlikely but very intriguing possibility: did Karl Ludwig Fleischmann find a way of getting a yeast species of disputed origin to Cincinnati, the trading and shipping capital of the West, roughly concurrent with the period when it was being introduced to the world by a confessed yeast thief in Germany? Could Over-the-Rhine hold co-equal billing with Germany for the first commercial production of lager beer? Unfortunately, this mystery is likely to remain a mystery. Like so many other buildings in Over-the-Rhine, Fleischmann's brewery and the mysteries that it could have unlocked were turned into a surface parking lot.

The first generally accepted location of a lagering cellar was located under the Lafayette Brewery at what is today 24 West McMicken Avenue. In the late 1820s, a French immigrant named Pierre (Peter) Jonte ran a combination cooperage and grocery. His cousin Frederich Billiod joined him in Cincinnati. He moved in with Jonte, and the two started a small brewery at the corner of Twelfth and Sycamore. In 1835, Billiod left to start the Lafayette Brewery. It burned in 1847 and was replaced with what is now the oldest brewery building in Over-the-Rhine. Like the Sohn and Jackson breweries down the street, the location of Lafayette abutting the hillside north of McMicken (then Hamilton Avenue) provided the opportunity to dig a "felsen," or lagering tunnel, into the hillside.

Regardless of who was the first, lager beer caught on quickly and transformed Over-the-Rhine and the city of Cincinnati. Lager's popularity corresponded with increasing waves of German immigration, the rapid construction of Over-the-Rhine and the explosive growth of a brewing industry that went from largely excluding German-Americans to being dominated by them. Opening a brewery on Vine Street between Thirteenth and Fourteenth Streets, Peter Noll joined the Bavarian Brewery as an early

Early and influential Cincinnati brewer Frederich Billiod opened the Lafayette Brewery on this site in 1835. In 1847, the wooden brewery building burned and was replaced with the brick structure on the right. The basement under this facility, extending into the hillside behind it, is believed to be the city's oldest lagering cellar.

pioneer of lager production. George Herancourt established his brewery on Hamilton Avenue in 1847. Johann Kauffman built his lager brewery in 1859. German immigrants Johann George Sohn and George Klotter established the Hamilton Brewery in 1845 (later the Sohn Brewing Company and Mohawk Brewing Company) and were producing lager a few years later. Learning to brew from his father-in-law, Frederich Billiod, German immigrant John Hauck started a brewery in 1863 that became one of the most beloved in the city.

German lagers were originally brewed primarily by German immigrants for German immigrants, but the beer started to gain broader popularity in the 1850s and quickly rose to prominence as Cincinnati's beer of choice. Due to the combination of the popularity of Cincinnati lager and an influx of German immigrants, the brewing industry increased threefold during the 1850s. Germans didn't just make up ground in brewing; they took over. Before the Civil War, there were at least eight breweries manufacturing traditional ales and porters. By 1872, the number making traditional English-style brews had declined to three out of a citywide total of twenty-six breweries.

The 1880s have been called the high-water mark of Cincinnati brewing. Also known for darker reasons as the "decade of disorder," broader social changes helped make this period the nineteenth-century pinnacle of local brewing. The end of the Civil War and pasteurization were two of these changes. The purpose of digging felsen tunnels is to reach cavelike temperatures. In Cincinnati, that means that felsen tunnels stay at roughly about fifty-five degrees throughout the year. This is not cool enough to keep lager beer fresh, but it is a good start. Prior to artificial refrigeration, ice and a system of running cold water, brine or ammonia through copper tubes along the walls and ceilings were used to bring these tunnels down to about forty degrees. In the South, warmer surface temperatures and hotter air inside the buildings would make felsen tunnels less useful, and ice was particularly scarce. This created a market for exporting Cincinnati beer, but there were limitations on export: bottling was expensive and labor intensive, and it was hard to keep the beer fresh. The same conditions that created the export market in the South also made it difficult to get the beer to the consumer, and the southern market was completely closed during part of the Civil War. In 1864, as the war was coming to a close, two scientists named Louis Pasteur and Claude Bernard made a tremendous scientific breakthrough in a process created for the purpose of preventing beer and wine from spoiling. Pasteurization became used to keep milk and an endless number of other products fresh, but its initial intended application was beer, and it worked. Beer could withstand longer trips and warmer conditions. Although 90 percent of beer produced in Cincinnati was consumed locally, exporting helped the larger breweries grow. Christian Moerlein praised the process of pasteurization, saying that it let his exported beer arrive "as fresh and sparkling in the torrid as in the temperate zone." The Cincinnati Chamber of Commerce noted that beer exports increased tenfold between 1863 and 1883, "until the beer of Cincinnati is now sold in all the cities and important towns of the South, and as far west as the Rocky Mountains." Moerlein, the city's most significant exporter, also addressed freshness by shipping barrels (rather than bottles) and having the beer bottled locally at destinations including New Orleans, Boston, Pensacola, Omaha, Canada, Puerto Rico, the Philippines, Panama and Cuba. The invention of the crown bottle cap solved additional problems with keeping exports fresh and made bottling more practical, but this did not occur until 1892.

Above: The Christian Moerlein Elm Street Brewery grew from a side business at the back of Christian Moerlein's blacksmith shop to the largest brewery in Ohio and one of the five largest in the United States, but it did not survive Prohibition. *Courtesy of the Christian Moerlein Brewery.*

Below: The large brew house was demolished in the 1930s, but the bottling plant and icehouse (pictured), as well as the barrelhouse, malt house, office and stable, remain.

CHRISTIAN MOERLEIN BREWERY PRODUCTION NUMBERS

YEAR	NUMBER OF BARRELS PRODUCED
1853	1,000
1860	20,000
1870	60,000
1880	100,000
1890	225,000

Experimental forms of artificial refrigeration have existed since the late 1700s, but dramatic improvements in the compression systems made mechanical refrigeration practical in the 1870s and 1880s. Although refrigerators were not affordable for average homeowners in the 1870s, mechanical refrigeration made good economic sense for brewers. Ice was expensive. Getting it from Lake Erie involved a long journey and shipping fees, and the river did not freeze frequently enough to make it a meaningful source in most years. Most ice had to come from the canal because it froze more readily. Since ice was valuable and unregulated, there was a mad rush to cut it when conditions were right. The canal was also filthy, but the biggest complaint surrounding ice remained price. A ton of ice typically fluctuated between $5.00 and $7.00 in the late 1800s, but a warm winter drove prices up to $12.00 a ton in 1874. The following year, Christian Moerlein bought the first ice machine in Cincinnati. It permitted the brewer to produce clean ice at $1.50 per ton. Although it cost roughly $16,000.00 to $18,000.00 annually to own and operate this type of machine, the investment was clearly worth it. Moerlein explained all of the ways that it improved his business: it cut labor costs $8,000.00 to $10,000.00 a year, saved space and was cleaner and decreased humidity from less melting ice; better reliability insured year-round production; it allowed fermentation in twelve to thirteen days as opposed to sixteen to eighteen; and it saved about $60,000.00 in ice costs. It would have been hard to argue with this list of advantages. Several other large brewers followed suit, and essentially every brewery in the city was using artificial refrigeration and ice machines by 1888.

Improved equipment, greater mechanization and changes in corporate law also played interrelated roles in transforming brewing in the 1870s and 1880s. By 1834, P. O'Reilly's Brewery and the Washington Brewery were both using steam engines in their operations. Not coincidentally, they

KREBS LITHO. CO. CINCINNATI.

Christian Moerlein (signature)

Christian Moerlein reached the state of Ohio near penniless and with a limited grasp of the English language. He dug ditches when he first arrived in the city of Cincinnati, began brewing beer in the back of his blacksmith shop and rose to build one of the five largest breweries in the United States. *From the collection of the Public Library of Cincinnati and Hamilton County.*

reported production numbers that were at least double those being reported by their six other competitors (100 to 125 barrels per week versus 50 to 60 barrels per week). Continuing technical innovations further mechanized and standardized the brewing process. An 1865 account of a new brewery engine marveled at its efficiency:

> *The engine is sixteen horse powers. It can, at the same time, grind the malt, sift it, throw it into the mash tub, let in boiling water that it has made to boil, stir up the malt and water, draw it off, pump it up stairs and throw it into the kettle, heat the kettle of liquid until it boils, throw it into the coolers, cool it, force and carry it off into vats, ferment it, chafe it, and draw off beer. With a little practice the engine could be taught to drink the beer.*

These modern marvels of the mid- to late nineteenth century allowed brewers with adequate capital to invest in equipment and expansion, cut costs and dramatically increase production levels. Output of beer increased from 354,000 barrels in 1870 to 656,000 barrels in 1880, and to 1,115,000 barrels in 1890 (35,700,000 gallons in 1890). This forced some of the smaller breweries out of business, but changes in the laws governing corporate organization and operation gave larger, more sophisticated brewers access to capital that could be used for expansion. Previously, breweries were basically family businesses. Operations often had two partners who combined their capital, but these were basic partnerships. There were no shareholders. Easier incorporation led a number of industries, including brewing, to shift from personally held businesses to corporations with access to shareholder capital. The major beer barons held majority shares, retained control and were primarily motivated to incorporate to limit personal liability and permit ownership to pass more easily to family members upon the deaths of the city's original generation of German brewers, but incorporation also provided the ability to raise significant funds quickly.

The maximum number of breweries in Cincinnati at once is often said to be thirty-six, in 1860. This comes from the 1860 *Williams Cincinnati Directory*. The problem with using this source for an exact count is the manner in which the directory handled brewery listings in 1860. It listed brewers as a professional category rather than listing breweries as a business type (as it did in other years). This makes it difficult to confirm that there were ever really thirty-six "breweries" in Cincinnati at one time. At least twenty-two of these listings are probably actual breweries, but not all thirty-six. The personal listing for three of these "brewers" shows their residence and business as the same addresses and lists their businesses as "coffee houses," meaning that they probably had small bars that they supplied with their own beer—somewhere between the modern equivalent of microbrew pubs and home-brewers. Two of the listings, plus one business not listed in the total thirty-six, called their operations some version of "brewery and malt house," and none of them still existed by 1861. Three have personal listings that seem to contradict the classification of "brewer" as profession, and two more list their profession as brewer but without a brewery employer or name, meaning that they may have been trained as brewers but were unemployed or trying to get operations started. Regardless of whether the maximum number of businesses calling themselves breweries was thirty-six or twenty-something, the higher number counted a lot of small operations that got left behind as beer became big business.

In 1834, the Washington Brewery was the height of mechanization, possibly producing as much as 6,500 barrels a year. By 1877, there were about a dozen breweries with at least double this production capacity, and the biggest ones were making a lot more than double. Christian Moerlein made 72,588 barrels of beer that year. Windish-Muhlhauser, its closest competitor, made 59,475. George Weber's Jackson Brewery produced 52,894 barrels, and John Kauffman's Vine Street Brewery rolled out 39,529. These production numbers made Moerlein the thirteenth-largest brewery in the United States. Windish-Muhlhauser was twentieth, and Jackson was twenty-fourth.

With the success of their businesses, Cincinnati's top brewers were anointed with the title of "beer barons." While these men did not reach the financial heights of the era's richest industrialists, they did become quite wealthy. At his death in 1897, Christian Moerlein had amassed personal assets worth over $1,500,000 (excluding the value of his corporate-owned brewery). Gottlieb Muhlhauser and John Hauck were both millionaires. Herman Lackman had a summer farm in Glendale with three hundred acres, but it was dwarfed by the eight-hundred-acre spread the Muhlhauser family maintained in Butler County.

Before lager, breweries were modest, simple structures. The brew house was typically two stories, often wood. Since grains and other brewing materials can be very flammable, and making beer required the use of a lot of open flames, one of the first improvements in brewery architecture was a shift toward brick. Now believed to be the city's oldest remaining brewery building, the former Lafayette brew house at 24 West McMicken was constructed in 1847 after the original, 1835 building was destroyed by fire. The lager period brought the need to build larger and deeper. Construction of Windish-Muhlhauser's Lion Brewery required months of digging to build twenty cellars and subbasements, "twelve of them 18 X 150 feet, eight of them eight by eighty feet," before the visible structure started to rise from the ground. Lion, built in 1866, is representative of a lot of the breweries built between roughly 1850 and 1870. It is built in Romanesque Revival–style architecture, similar to the original brew house of the Bellevue Brewery, the Jackson Brewery, the 1869 portion of the Kauffman Brewery and the long-razed Christian Moerlein brew house. In the 1870s and 1880s, the breweries got both larger and more elaborate. Lion expanded significantly but kept consistent design elements. Others began building more ornate, architecturally significant additions. The Banner Brewery both expanded with an ornate addition and erected a decorative cupola on its existing building. The Gerke Brewery hired a renowned architect to redesign its brewery as one of the city's most beautiful pieces of architecture. (Although Gerke used the designs in ads as an illustration of its brewery, the designs may never have actually been built.) Kauffman's 1880s brew house has hops carved into its stone details. Sohn Brewery's 1886 expansion is the most ornamental brewery building remaining, featuring cherubs toasting beers and a brewer's star of beer purity at its crown.

By the close of the 1880s, the city's twenty-three breweries had an undeniable impact on the city's economy, and these economic engines had become almost exclusively located in the German neighborhoods of Over-the-Rhine, Mohawk-Brighton (now mostly considered OTR) and the German northeast sections of the West End. The Christian Moerlein Brewery employed 500 men, Windish-Muhlhauser another 200. The numerous smaller breweries like the John Hauck Brewery commonly employed between 75 and 150 men. In addition to direct employment,

The Windish-Muhlhauser Lion Brewery is pictured on the right of the canal, in years before significant expansion. Lion was one of the city's largest breweries. After Prohibition, it became the home of the Burger Brewing Company. Located on the southwest corner of Liberty and Central Parkway, part of the brewery remains behind the Cincinnati Ballet. *Courtesy of the Cincinnati Historical Society Library, Cincinnati Museum Center.*

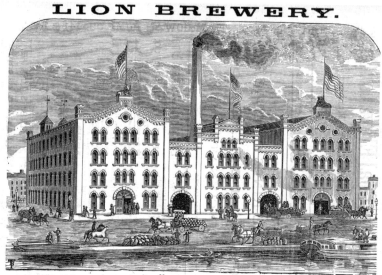

A Lion Brewery ad shows the expanded facility as it appeared in the 1880s. *From the collection of the Public Library of Cincinnati and Hamilton County.*

brewing supported a large number of related industries. Cincinnati had four hops dealers and nine malt houses. Brewers were a significant source of income for some of the city's 52 coopers, who in turn supported four businesses that supplied cooperage equipment and materials. Iron and brass foundries, including one owned by brewer George Klotter, made felsen tunnel cooling lines, stair rails, structural members for breweries and brass taps, faucets and fittings for transporting and serving beer. John Schmelzer & Son, with its business located on the canal, was a successful manufacturer of beer faucets and beer pumps and had competition from the John H. McGowan Co. on Central Avenue. There were two malt kiln manufacturers in Over-the-Rhine and a third on Pearl Street. There were dozens of businesses that made bottles and provided bottling supplies. Brewers would have been good customers of some of the city's twenty-nine grain dealers and its thirteen refrigeration specialists.

Of course, there were also thousands of Cincinnatians employed in the profession of selling Cincinnati beer, and there was seemingly no shortage to the number of people wanting a drink or the number of places where

GEORGE GERKE. President.
RORT. M. KUERZE, Sec'y and Treas,   South-east Cor. Canal and Plum Street.

In the 1870s and 1880s, successful, growing and increasingly incorporated breweries began placing more emphasis on the quality and detail of their brewery architecture. The buildings themselves became a significant part of the brewery's image, frequently the centerpiece of their advertising. Gerke, located at what would now be the southeast corner of Plum Street and Central Parkway, immediately south of the canal, was an example of Cincinnati's world-class brewery architecture. The entire brewery has been razed. *From the collection of the Public Library of Cincinnati and Hamilton County.*

they could buy one. Roughly three-fifths of beer produced in Cincinnati in 1890 was consumed here by its 297,000 residents. In 1893, Americans consumed an average sixteen gallons of beer per capita, but in Cincinnati the average was forty gallons for every man, woman and child in the city—two and a half times the national average. Cincinnatians loved beer, and while ethnic distinctions remained, by the 1860s the German love for a good beer was being enjoyed far beyond the boundaries of the German communities. In 1889, the city had 1,841 saloons, four hilltop resorts and hundreds of restaurants that also served beer, and beer was a central part of the experience at dozens of bowling alleys, over a dozen theatres, a professional baseball team and a world-class zoological garden.

The beauty and expense of brewery building architecture in the late nineteenth century was a reflection of the success of the breweries, and they served a role as an extension of the brand. Advertisements of the time feature etchings of the buildings (sometimes exaggerating their size or architectural details). It may have also been an attempt to gain respect. The same travel guides that had spoken highly of Over-the-Rhine in the 1870s largely glossed over it by the mid-1880s, advising visitors to head to the zoo and hilltop resorts, but these publications continued to praise "the great breweries, for which Cincinnati has become so renowned." They were called an "astonishment to everybody." What these breweries made, who drank their beer and where they drank it were far more controversial topics. After the Civil War, German-style lager beer became America's drink of choice, but both its popularity and its inextricable link to German immigrants made it the primary target of temperance advocates and a growing number of prohibitionists.

After Prohibition the brewery formerly operated as Sohn and Mohawk became the Clyffside Brewery. At the time this photo was taken, the Sohn home still stood, but it was demolished to provide for construction of a 1937 addition. *Courtesy of Steven Hampton, president, Brewery District CURC.*

Cincinnati Breweries in 1889	Location
Adam Henry Brewery	Camp Washington, on the canal
Banner Brewery (aka Weyand Brewing Co.)	OTR, northeast corner of Canal and Walnut
Bellevue Brewery	Mohawk-Brighton (OTR), on the canal
John C. Bruckmann Brewery	Cumminsville, on the canal
Foss Schneider Brewing Co.	West End, Freeman Ave.
Gambrinus Stock	OTR, 12th (then Abigail) and Sycamore
Gerke Brewing Company	Corner of Plum and Canal, immediately south of OTR
Germania Brewing Co.	Mohawk-Brighton (OTR), on the canal
John Hauck Brewing Company	West End, Dayton Street
Herancourt Brewing Co.	Fairmount
Hudepohl & Kotte Buckeye Brewery	OTR, East Clifton (then Buckeye)
George Weber's Jackson Brewery	OTR, 208 Mohawk
Jung Brewing Co. (aka Western Brewery)	West End, Freeman Ave.
John Kauffman Brewing Co.	OTR, 1622 Vine St.
Herman Lackman Brewery	Queensgate, West 6th
Windish-Muhlhauser Lion Brewery	SW corner of Liberty and Central Pkwy. (then the canal, immediately west of OTR)
Christian Moerlein Elm Street Brewing Co.	OTR, Elm Street, Henry, McMicken, Dunlap
Klinckhamer & Sons Park Brewery	OTR, SE corner of 13th and Race
Queen City Brewery	West End, Freeman Ave.
Schaller Bros. Main Street Brewery	OTR, 1622–1630 Main Street

CINCINNATI BREWERIES IN 1889	LOCATION
Schmidt & Bro.	OTR, 132–134 and 125 E. McMicken
J.G. Sohn & Co. Brewery	OTR, 244 W. McMicken
J. Walker Brewing Co.	OTR, corner of Liberty and Sycamore

DRUNKENNESS AND BLOODSHED
The Parallel Perspective

In the 1875 tome *History of the Great Temperance Reforms*, Reverend James Shaw uses the "science" of the day to conclude that "[a]bout ninety per cent of the suffering, pauperism and crime in Europe and America come from intemperance." He blamed alcohol for the destruction of families: "The drunkard's *children* are left often without food, clothes, care or support, grow up as tender plants of disease, wretchedness, poverty and disorder." He blamed it for nations losing military battles, arguing that drunken sailors sink ships. He blamed it for mental illness: "[T]he drunkard not only injures and enfeebles his own nervous system, but entails mental disease upon his family. His daughters are nervous and hysterical, his sons are weak, wayward and eccentric, and sink insane under the pressure of excitement." He blamed it for taxation and the increased need for social services: "As intemperance inevitably leads to poverty, so poverty must end in *Pauperism*." He blamed it for dumbing down society: "The habits of the parents of three-hundred of the idiots were learned, and one-hundred-and-forty-five, or nearly *one-half*, are reported as known to be habitual drunkards. The parents of cases sixty-two were drunkards and had *seven idiotic children*." He even blamed it for cholera, noting that a Glasgow doctor claimed that in a recent cholera outbreak only 19 percent of temperate patience died, compared to 91.2 percent of drinkers. And, of course, he blamed alcohol for almost all crime: alcohol "prepares the way for the commission of crime of every kind, and for those which require a steady hand and a clear head, there is need of the paralyzing effect of the alcohol upon the conscience and moral sense, and that such an effect is desired and sought by the professional criminal is a fact well known…Enraged tigers and hideous vipers could roam our streets more safely than human beings so poisoned and crazed by strong drink."

While Shaw and fellow temperance crusaders oversimplified complicated social factors and often confused correlation with causation, they were responding to dramatic and undeniable changes in society. People drank in early America. In fact, by 1830, the average American male was consuming more than four times the amount of liquor consumed today, mostly in the form of whiskey or hard cider. Alcohol was considered healthy, "particularly for digestive ills." Parents put sugar in it to make it sweet for sick children. In early Cincinnati, many people drank nothing *but* alcoholic beverages. Coffee and tea were luxury items, and milk and water were often diseased. As Cincinnati entered the 1840s, it was not the amount of alcohol that people drank that changed. What changed was who drank it and how they drank it.

Between 1800 and 1860, the number of cities in America with more than ten thousand inhabitants grew from six to ninety-three. During the mid-nineteenth century, America went from an agrarian nation to one more heavily dominated by a new form of urban life. This brought dramatic changes in family and social structures. In earlier agrarian America, people lived and worked on the same plot of land, with their families. Most of the population only traveled to town periodically and for necessary reasons. They might come into contact with the occasional Swede or German, but they were primarily Anglo-Saxon Protestant. Men commonly drank alcohol, but they did it during the workday and in family settings. Public intoxication was a rare site, and so was crime.

Significant immigration occurred from Germany and Ireland during the period when Cincinnati was the most important city in the western lands. Cincinnati was transformed in a relatively short period of time, and it lacked precedence or infrastructure for handling it. Cincinnati's saloon-to-resident ratio remained both high and relatively constant throughout the nineteenth century. In 1834, it had approximately 223 saloons and taverns, or roughly one for every thirty-eight males over the age of fifteen. In 1890, the number of saloons had grown to 1,810 but the population was 297,000, meaning about one saloon for every forty-one adult males. However, the face of drinking changed. Early drinking establishments were taverns. These places typically served food and had lodging for travelers. Saloons, also commonly called "dram-shops," "ale houses," "porter houses" or "coffee houses," were different from taverns. They were purely urban institutions, catering to the

Drunkenness and Bloodshed

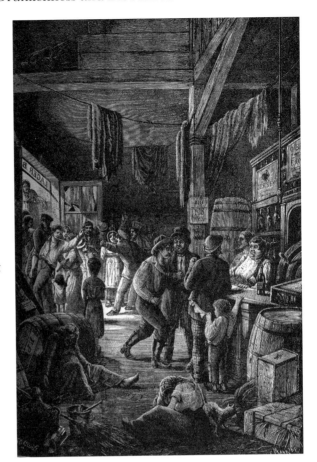

Right: Temperance publications depicted all saloons as houses of vice and debauchery, portraying neglected children, ruined women and violence. *From the collection of the Public Library of Cincinnati and Hamilton County.*

Below: A depiction of life inside Wielert's, where women and children were welcome and safe, with the symphony playing in the background. *Courtesy of Steven Hampton, president, Brewery District CURC.*

urban working class. Saloons added the bar to bars—a place where you could stand and have a drink (or several) by the glass.

As waves of immigrants arrived in the city to seek industrial labor positions, Cincinnati saloons became increasingly associated with the city's German and Irish populations. Temperance had always had ethnic, religious and socioeconomic biases. The ethnic and religious biases remained fairly constant, but there was some shift in the socioeconomic makeup. Early temperance movements were characterized by the affluent attempting to impose moderation on the unruly working class, but by the mid-1800s, the face of temperance had become solidly middle class. What remained constant was its white Anglo-Saxon, usually native-born makeup. The movement also tended to glorify rural life and demonize cities. The connection between immigrant groups, new patterns of drinking and some legitimate complaints about city life led many to agree with local and notable temperance advocate Samuel Carry when he called Germans the "disorganizers of society."

Protest against alcohol use and immigration cannot be dismissed in the 1800s as purely xenophobic or puritanical. There were legitimate social problems associated with both immigration and drinking, and they often went together. In 1819, Cincinnati's combined German and Irish population had been 10 percent. By 1840, it had risen to 34 percent after an explosion of the population. Although the Irish waterfront was far more impoverished, dirty and violent than the German neighborhoods, Over-the-Rhine rapidly accumulated its own populations of unskilled immigrants in increasing congestion, and many native Cincinnatians painted all immigrants with the same brush. In the later half of the nineteenth century, new arrivals were increasingly unskilled and impoverished. This forced increases in city welfare spending. Immigrants also violated general customs and liquor laws, most notably drinking openly on Sundays. This was the case since at least the 1830s, but it became a bigger bugaboo among the puritanical set as greater numbers of immigrants and a growing acceptability of public drinking made it more visible after the Civil War. Saloons were also a matter of contention. While the vast majority of saloons throughout the city seem to have been congenial, social places, many did maintain prostitutes, and some in places like Irish "Rat Town" were likely the common scenes of extraordinary violence. Regardless of their orderliness, it had to constantly rub temperance advocates the wrong way as they walked through areas like Over-the-Rhine where there was a saloon every few feet.

Most complaints against the immigrant populations combined a basis in fact with irrational conclusions. After Cincinnati German singing societies held a singing festival in 1849, a subsequent cholera epidemic was blamed on the Germans. Nineteenth-century German historian Emil Klauprecht observed that this was "an opinion accepted by a lot of bigots." No matter how off-key, German singing does not give people cholera. However, crowded tenement housing with inadequate access to fresh water does contribute to both the outbreak and spread of disease. While the worst living conditions were reserved for the Irish and African Americans, living conditions would have gotten progressively worse in Over-the-Rhine as the open fields and freshwater canal of 1830 became one of the nation's most densely populated neighborhoods—bordered by an open sewer. Crime increased dramatically in the mid- to late 1800s, and immigrants did begin to constitute a higher percentage of offenders. In 1845, there were only 873 arrests in all of Hamilton County. In 1853, there were 6,769 arrests just within Cincinnati's borders; and as crime rose, so did the percentage of immigrants being arrested. In 1845, immigrants constituted 28 percent of Hamilton County's jail population. The percentage rose to 54 percent in three years and hit 65 percent in 1863. Some of this was attributable to changes in policing, but most reflected an actual rise in criminal behavior.

Any criminal behavior that fed the stereotype of drunken, violent immigrants was a feather in the hat of temperance and prohibition advocates. In 1884, they were handed an ostrich feather. Crime was big headlines in Cincinnati. Murder, rape and robbery seemed commonplace. In part, this was attributable to reasons that sound familiar today. Cincinnati had close to a dozen English- and German-language newspapers in the 1880s that all had to compete with one another for audiences. Papers had already learned the adage "if it bleeds it leads" and routinely reported on grisly crimes regardless of where they occurred. This exacerbated accurate perception in Cincinnati that the criminal justice system was terminally flawed. The city only had a few dozen police officers, many of whom future Governor Foraker would describe as having "a bad reputation" because "[a]mong them were some who had been convicted of crimes, and others who…were charged not only with connivance at crime but with the actual commission of crime while on duty." Cincinnati cops were known to rob people at gunpoint while wearing their uniforms. Trials took unnecessarily long periods to occur after indictment, often long enough that witnesses disappeared or failed to recollect events. Charges were often dropped by judges without findings of fact or legitimate cause. Juries simply failed to convict obviously guilty people, and when convictions occurred, sentences were often remarkably light. Charges of corruption, bribery and incompetence ran rampant. All the while, the papers continued to churn out stories of grisly crimes, and they did not always have to go far from home to get them. In one particularly heinous example in 1883, an Avondale family was butchered so that the killer could sell their corpses to a medical college for dissection. Killing people for salable product to medical colleges or using dissection as a means of getting rid of the bodies of murder victims was either so common, or at least believed to be so common, that state law prohibited medical colleges from accepting bodies that showed marks of violence without notifying the coroner.

At a time when the public was outraged at crime run amok, a senseless murder was committed on Christmas Eve 1883. Two stable hands, William Berner, described as "a young German," and Joseph Palmer, "a light mulatto," murdered their employer, William Kirk. Mr. Kirk was savagely beaten and strangled to death. His body was tossed into the back of a wagon, taken to the outskirts of town and dumped in a thicket of bushes. The motive was $285 that Kirk had earned on the sale of a horse. After apprehension, the killers demonstrated no signs of remorse. Berner confessed no less than seven times and admitted that the plan had been hatched weeks in advance. The crime was a clear example of first-degree murder, a capital offense—a hanging offense—but Cincinnatians had good reason to believe that justice would be denied.

The system didn't seem to be working, and there was immediate public speculation in the Berner case about the relationship between the defense attorney and his former law partner, the presiding judge. All of the speculation surrounding the trial was heightened when Berner's attorney had the trial bifurcated, meaning that Berner and Palmer would be tried separately. Berner was going to be tried first. To many, the writing on the wall was clear: the young German would be acquitted and the black guy would hang for the crime of both men. No one seems to have been bothered by the fact that Palmer was likely to hang, but the public turned pretrial speculation into irrefutable proof that the justice system was inept and corrupt. This sentiment had merit. A total of 504 men were called in jury selection in order to adequately handpick a jury of 12. Jury selection had been dragged on so long that it was said to have cost the state $5,000, and

Berner's father reportedly paid the defense attorney $4,500, a legal fee that drew outrage in 1884.

As the trial got underway, it became a primary topic in beer gardens and saloons. Saloon windows displayed caricatures of the jury and the attorneys with derogatory and violent captions. Rumors of bribery, collusion between the attorneys and judge and jury tampering ran rampant. Booze and trial news were being blended in an increasingly combustible cocktail.

Rather than capital murder, Berner was convicted of mere manslaughter on March 27, 1884. The jurors left the courthouse marked men. One of the jurors was badly "beaten by a number of his acquaintances," and a juror from Harrison fled his home. Another juror was fired from his job, and his co-workers spent the lunch hour hanging his effigy. The jury foreman went into hiding. A public meeting was called at Central Turner Hall that evening, and a larger public meeting was planned for the following day, the day of sentencing. At roughly 2:00 p.m. on Friday, March 28, 1884, Berner was sentenced to twenty years in prison for the confessed brutal, capital murder.

Organized primarily by affluent and respected Cincinnati citizens, an open meeting was held at Music Hall later that evening. The planned speeches mostly addressed the need for judicial reform: different rules for jury selection, methods for processing criminal cases faster and higher ethical standards for lawyers and judges. The large audience was polite during the speeches and the meeting was orderly, but violence was the clear undertone. "Ropes suitable for a lynching party were openly displayed and threats of mob violence were frequently heard." The meeting concluded mildly with a resolution for legal reforms, but as soon as the crowd of between six and eight thousand frustrated citizens made their way out to Elm Street, a loud call arose: "To the jail!"

Some people carried lynching ropes, some acquired stones or other weapons, some just went along out of curiosity about what was going to happen. There was no clear leadership, just thousands of agitated citizens making their way from Over-the-Rhine to the county jail, built immediately adjacent to the courthouse (both essentially located where the courthouse and Justice Center are today). The group accumulated more curious marchers as it proceeded. At the time a crowd of thousands reached the jail, it was staffed only by the sheriff and a handful of deputies. Joists, crowbars and hammers were used to gain entry into the jail office through an iron basement door. Fearing that a violent response to the crowd would make the situation worse, the sheriff had ordered his men not to fire on the crowd. This permitted them to continue to pry through the interior iron doors separating the office from the spiral stone stairwell up to the cells. Members of the mob made their way freely through the jail, demanding that prisoners tell them where Berner and Palmer could be found.

Fortunately for Berner, he had already been taken from the jail to be put on a train to the state prison in Columbus. This protected him from the Cincinnati lynch mob, but he almost fell into the hands of one in Loveland. Stopped awaiting documents and a transfer, an angry mob tried to take Berner from police custody for summary justice, but the crowd mistook one of the deputies for Berner, jumped him and started beating him severely. This provided Berner with the opportunity to escape. While the streets of Cincinnati were already stained with blood, Berner was "coolly enjoying a game of cards...unaware of the riot" when he was reapprehended by Cincinnati detectives and a Loveland marshal on the following Saturday afternoon. The mob in Cincinnati was ignorant of both Berner's transfer and his escape. The sheriff advised the crowd that he had been transported, but his words were interpreted as a ploy to drive the crowd away.

Palmer, on the other hand, remained in the jail, vulnerable to mob lynching. He seems to have survived the night due largely to his own steely, sociopathic nerve. Apparently a very light-skinned man, when the mob approached his cell and demanded that he verify his identity as the accused Palmer, he responded: "No, can't you see that I am a white man?" The calm of his reply under the circumstances was sufficient to cause the group to pass on to other cells. None of the prisoners was harmed during the time that the crowd was roaming through the jail. There were twenty-three murder suspects incarcerated at the time, including the alleged murderer of the Avondale family. Reports vary about whether the intentions of the crowd included lynching all of them or just Berner. Since there was no leadership, it is likely that the intentions and purpose of the group varied by individual.

Fifteen city police officers arrived as backup but were pushed out of the way by the crowd. A little before 10:00 p.m., the riot alarm was sounded. This brought more police backup and the local militia, but it also had the effect of drawing more members of the mob—a group that may have reached as many as ten thousand people. When the mob made its way back into the jail, the militia shot a volley of blank cartridges in hopes of scattering the rioters. The riot alarm also led to the evening's first casualties. Additional police officers made their way through the crowds and into the jail by entering the courthouse on Main Street and coming through the underground tunnel that connected the buildings. The policemen shouted out who they were as they came through the tunnel, but edgy and now using live ammunition, militiamen shot at least five of their brethren. The militia later blamed the shootings on rioters, but officers who lived through it confirmed that the militia fired the shots.

Still believing that Berner was inside, the mob tried to burn the jail by lighting adjacent wood buildings on fire, trying to force the evacuation of the jail, and made continued attempts to regain entry. Friday night's fires were ultimately extinguished. Unaware that the sheriff had ordered his men to refrain from firing on the crowd, or that the militia was initially using blanks, the mob looted gun stores and hardware stores, stripping them of rifles, powder and ammunition. A cannon was taken from the city's largest gun store and paraded down Main Street by a group of about fifty people, led by fife and drum. Rioters busted out the jail's windows with rocks and started firing pistols into it. Police and militia started firing back. The sheriff gave orders to shoot above the crowd to try to disperse them. The sheriff seems to have remained a steady voice of discipline and restraint, but he had limited control in a confusing chain of command that helped exacerbate the situation. The sheriff only controlled the jail building and his deputies. County commissioners claimed jurisdiction over the courthouse building. The chief of police, who was also present, gave orders to his men that could contradict the ones that Colonel Hunt gave the militia or that the sheriff gave his deputies. During most of the riot, the mayor was too ill to get out of bed. The militia ignored the sheriff's instructions and started firing directly into the crowd. At roughly 1:30 a.m., a seventeen-year-old laborer named Lew Kent fell dead in the street, shot through the brain by a militiaman's bullet. He was the first murdered civilian but far from the last. At a little after 2:00 a.m., a man named Newton Cobb from Manchester, Ohio, was shot in the shoulder by soldiers firing from inside the jail. He may have been the first casualty described as a "bystander," but by 2:30 a.m. two more people described as "bystanders" were seriously shot, and three more lay dying of bullet wounds. Militia justified firing indiscriminately on people in the street by claiming that they were trying to prevent the jail from being burned or blown up by groups that were pushing drums of coal oil into the entryway. As the crowd started to thin out around 3:00 a.m., the militia emerged from the jail and started firing at people who were running away. Police then roamed the streets in armed patrols for the remainder of the early morning hours. Using overturned carriages, furniture, sandbags and whatever was available, barricades were hastily erected around the jail in all directions. Another war had erupted on the banks of Cincinnati's Rhine.

On Friday, a mob wanted to lynch two murderers. As nefarious as this motivation may have been, at least it was consistent with a protest over rampant crime, political corruption and lax law enforcement. The motives were different on Saturday, less defined and dramatically more ironic. On Saturday, the motive was revenge. The crowds wanted to make the militia and law enforcement pay for the blood spilled during their sloppy attempts to maintain law and order on the previous night.

A large crowd started to form early on Saturday. "All day long Saturday, the militia and police were on duty, and the court-house and jail were surrounded by tired-out but determined men." No blood was shed during daylight hours, but crowds built throughout the day. The crowds grew larger and more aggressive as dusk gave way to the darkness of a new moon and Saturday night began. A witness noted that "[t]he mob is greater than last night and there are more drunken men in it." By nightfall, the jail and courthouse were surrounded by a sea of people stretching blocks in every direction. As motives became more amorphous and newspapers were reporting Berner's escape from custody in Loveland, what building was attacked may have become less relevant. More importantly, all three sides of the jail had been heavily barricaded, but no barricades had been erected in front of the adjacent courthouse. At roughly 9:00 p.m., "[t]he riot began with the throwing of boulders and brick-bats at the Court-house, while some fired pistols and shot-guns at the windows." The crowd battered down the iron front door of the building. As one group was attacking the door, another entered the treasurer's office, located on the northwest corner of the building, by breaking into a basement window. This group broke up furniture, covered it in coal oil and set the courthouse on fire. The courthouse and jail were only connected by the underground tunnel, and there was a yard between them, so burning the courthouse seems to have had no motive beyond general destruction. Among a wealth of other articles of public interest, the building was said to have contained one of the most extensive and historic law libraries in the United States. As the courthouse slowly burned, rioters began shooting at the militia and policemen who made attempts to douse the fire. The police and militia shot back. Death started to accumulate. Periodically, someone from the crowd would wave a white flag, move from haphazard safety positions in doorways or behind buildings or barricades and drag the dead or dying off the battlefields of Main, Court and Sycamore Streets.

Earlier in the day, as violence appeared eminent, the governor called out National Guard regiments from across Ohio. The Fourth Regiment from Dayton was the first to arrive a little after 9:00 p.m., but when they glimpsed the extent of the brutal, senseless bloodshed, they turned around, walked back to the train station and returned to Dayton. Regiments from Springfield and Columbus were more useful. Arriving about 10:00 p.m. on Saturday, they drove the crowd farther from the courthouse. This gave the fire department the space necessary to save the northwest corner of the building, which contained some of the public records. Out-of-town militia also stepped up the violence. Their arrival led to "men being mowed down like grass under the keen sweep of a scythe." The police department's Gatling gun was brought out to hold the line, but its only role on Saturday was intimidation. There may have been consternation by law enforcement about using a weapon that could fire a constant rain of bullets on a crowd of fellow citizens, but restraint with the Gatling gun did not stop the growing number of casualties. Initially, Saturday's dead were taken to a nearby restaurant. When its tables were filled with the dead, dying and seriously wounded, casualties were taken to Burdsal's drugstore on Main Street. When it had accumulated its maximum number of bodies, a saloon on Ninth Street became the temporary morgue. By midnight on Saturday, a witness noted: "Such a night of blood as this has not before darkened the history of Cincinnati." The areas around Court and Canal were a literal war zone, with seemingly countless Cincinnatians willing to sacrifice their lives for no clear or rational purpose. A journalist wrote that for "some unaccountable motive the mob stands in the streets in range of soldiers' guns, apparently courting death." Kinzbach's drugstore, at the corner of Court and Walnut, became the next business converted into a morgue when the other locations could hold no more bodies.

Groups of men went searching for weapons. A crowd moved through the night down Main Street. Their target was William & Powell & Co.'s gun store. They brought barrels of coal oil that they intended to use to burn through the storefront. This plan was thwarted by the owner and his clerks. They were hiding inside the gun store—well armed. Five rioters were shot, and the rest retreated. Another group took two cannons from Music Hall, but police recaptured the guns while the rioters were still trying to find powder to fire them.

Sunday was a day of apprehension. It was rumored that city hall and Music Hall would both be the targets of mob violence. Police and militia camped out in city hall in preparation for a standoff. Nationwide, people watched bulletin boards and news wires for updates on the fate of Cincinnati. City streets within firing range of the courthouse were deserted. Barricades had been added on Main and Court Streets on the courthouse side. Sunday's violence reached murder pitch faster than the day before when a man was shot by militia in Over-the-Rhine, probably from behind the newly erected barricades on the Main Street bridge. This was the first daylight shooting. Most of the day was spent by groups tossing stones at the police and militia and shouting insults. One of the taunts was reportedly, "Wait till to-night!

In a scene that must have been reminiscent of the 1855 election riots, militiamen and city police man a barricade at the Main Street bridge over the canal. *Courtesy of the Cincinnati Historical Society Library, Cincinnati Museum Center.*

Wait till to-night! Wait till we get good and drunk and we'll hoist you blue coated men behind your barrels!" The Gatling gun was put into actual service for the first time. By roughly 8:00 p.m., gunfire had begun at the courthouse, described as "heavier than at anytime last night." Just trying to cross the street blocks away from the courthouse, one of the city's wealthiest pork barons was caught by a bullet from the Gatling gun at the corner of Ninth and Main.

There were also signs that mayhem was spreading. A man had been murdered on Fountain Square on Saturday afternoon. A group broke into Music Hall to try to take cannons and was driven off by militia. A group of men or boys was shoving streetcars off the track. Another group went to lynch one of the Berner jurors but abandoned the plan when he wasn't at home.

Hundreds more militiamen were coming in from all over the state of Ohio. Cincinnati businesses were closed. The typical revelry of a Sunday afternoon was replaced with quiet streets. Beer gardens and saloons were shuttered. After the first use of the Gatling gun at 8:00 p.m., it was fired periodically at random down the street to keep the streets clear and prevent the accumulation of rioters. It worked. There were now between 2,500 and 3,000 militiamen guarding the courthouse, and the federal government had issued the approval to dispatch federal troops. The governor then gave the order for any and all remaining guardsmen not already in Cincinnati to go there with haste. Rumors of continued violence, conspiracies, plans for organized attacks and forces being marshaled in Kentucky or Turner Hall were rampant, but none transpired into action. Three days of rioting were concluded with an overwhelming show of force. Initially, there was fear that violence would re-erupt as soon as troops were withdrawn, but that did not occur. Monday, March 31, was quiet all day and evening.

Peace was restored, but nothing was solved. At least 45 people had been killed, and a known 123 were injured. Actual injuries were estimated to be in the hundreds, with only the most serious cases seeking help. Some changes to the criminal justice system followed the riots, but they were modest. Significant changes in police qualifications, training and ethics were implemented. A renewed sense of law and order was said to have fallen over the city and the use of capital punishment increased, but the riots and looting also attracted a number of criminals from other cities. This apparently attributed to a notable rise in crime following the riots.

William Berner was a model prisoner who accumulated "good time gained" and was released from custody on June 5, 1895. He would have been roughly twenty-nine years old upon his release. Berner's defense attorney was charged with "bribery and subordination" for his role in the trial but was acquitted.

While no one seems to have bothered arguing that the riots solved anything, a great deal of time and effort was spent looking for who and what to blame for their occurrence. The press was blamed, and they deserved it. Before the riots, the *Cincinnati Enquirer* had suggested "that the temporary elevation of Judge Lynch to the bench seemed necessary and therefore justifiable." Lawyers were also blamed with both justification and overstatement. Although not absolute, there were ethnic and socioeconomic differences in opinion about the militia. The German-language press placed primary blame on the militia for causing Saturday's and Sunday's violence by indiscriminately firing on the crowd who were unarmed on Friday night. Some English-language commentators took the opposite tack, concluding that no one in the Friday night crowd was truly innocent and suggesting that the sheriff should have immediately called out the Gatling gun and established order with merciless, murderous force

Of all the hindsight dissection, the most extensive was a book-length, rambling, preaching diatribe called *The Cincinnati Riot: Its Causes and Results*, published in 1886. In it, author J.S. Tunison goes through a number of these causes and observations and adds extensive criticism of the political process and machine politics but ultimately places most of the blame on one culprit above all others: beer.

It was said on Saturday that "excitement in the city grew hourly, especially in that part of the city over the canal." People feared that Saturday would be particularly bloody because it was payday and Sunday was a day off of work for many—the recipe for drunken disorder. Observers noted that more people appeared noticeably intoxicated on Saturday evening, and it was clearly the bloodiest, most destructive and baffling low point in three days of carnage. Although stolen just like weapons from the armory and private gun stores, forty of the rifles used by rioters were procured from Central Turner Hall. Unlike any other source of stolen guns, this (at least temporarily) led to a rumor that the Turners were entering the riot as an organized force. It did not go unnoticed that although the list of names of the rioters killed and wounded include some Anglo-Saxon surnames, a smattering of O'Day,

Sullivan and McHugh and several described as "colored," a disproportionate amount of the casualties had names like Breitenbach, Westenhoff and Vogelgesang. If the fallen are a representative sample of the crowd, German-American laborers composed most of it, particularly on Saturday night; and among the very few victims with professional qualifications were two brewers.

Like the May 4, 1886 Haymarket affair in Chicago, there seems to have been some discussion in Cincinnati about the notion of a "blood disease," the idea that some ethnic groups—like Germans—were less capable of functioning in democracies and were prone to anarchy. *The Cincinnati Riot* took a more nuanced and paternalistic tone. While Tunison concluded that Cincinnati's German-American community was responsible for "demoralizing the youth of other nationalities" and making "vice rampant and unblushing," his solution was not specifically anti-German. In Tunison's view, Cincinnati had good, productive German-Americans. The fact that the rioters were primarily German did not reflect badly on what Tunison called "the better classes of German people."

The solution was not to root out the immigrants but to root out the forces that corrupted them: "People are ruled more than they would be willing to confess by example, and what Cincinnati needs now, and for years to come, will be an example of conservatism in social affairs, in politics, in art and in morals." Specifically, Cincinnati showed a lack of religious observation. This was particularly apparent in the amount of drinking that occurred on Sundays, and seemingly above all else, Tunison blamed the riots on lax enforcement of Sunday liquor laws:

> *Through its history, the city has shown a remarkable respect for all laws except the so-called Sunday liquor laws. The experiment made with these have shown that such legislation, so far as one city in the United States is concerned, is worse than useless, because, by producing laws which cannot be enforced, it tends to bring all law into contempt…The morality of the whole city has been so vitiated by the German proletarian view of things, that the people as a whole have nothing to do with the conduct of the individual, that, in short, freedom in a free country means the license to be as wicked, as injurious to society, as disgusting in personal habits as the most immoral and reckless persons may choose to be. If that is freedom in a free country, commend us to a despotism where such human beings as these have to be vaccinated, whether they are willing or not.*

Tunison also blamed machine politics, but he blamed machine politics on working-class Germans: "It is useless to deny or conceal the fact that Cincinnati is at the mercy of a proletariat hardly less vicious than that which controls New York. The difference is that the proletariat in one case is Celtic in the other Teutonic." Ironically, the city's reaction to a genuinely, clearly corrupt Democratic city government gave rise to the most notorious era of machine politics under Republican Party "Boss" Cox.

The courthouse riot in 1884 was one of the bloodiest and most senseless urban riots in the nation's history. It represented the culmination of decades of disorder and social decay, and Tunison spoke for many when he laid the blame for all the havoc on drunkenness. At a time when the city contained about two thousand saloons, breweries were producing previously unimaginable amounts of beer, brewing had become one of the city's most important industries, whiskey was one of the biggest exports and the seven-day-a-week revelry in Over-the-Rhine seemed nonstop, it was a mistake to conclude that prohibition forces were down for the count. Rather, they were building up ammunition.

SIDE-DOOR SUNDAYS
IN THE PARIS OF AMERICA

In 1831, the State of Ohio passed a statute that read: "Whoever sells or barters any spirituous liquors on the first day of the week, commonly called Sunday, shall be fined not more than $5.00." With some modifications primarily aimed at making it more stringent and increasing the fines, this remained the letter of the law for the next eighty-nine years.[4] It also started a long Cincinnati tradition: ignoring the Sunday closing law.

A *de facto* policy that essentially let an entire city ignore state law created challenges for politicians and the police. The spring of 1878 exemplifies how the unofficial policy worked. On April 6, 1878, city government issued the following decree:

> *To the officers and men of the Police Force:*
>
> *You will see to it that the law in regard to performing common labor on Sunday is enforced hereafter more rigidly. Officers will instruct their men to close up all billiard rooms, stop pool-playing, the rolling of nine pins, and such theaters and variety shows as are patronized by disorderly or disreputable characters. After notification to close their places, should they fail to do so, you will make arrests and bring the offenders before court.*

---

4. The City of Cincinnati's original ordinances, passed in 1828, also prohibited the sale of alcohol on Sundays "except to a traveler on a journey or to a family in case of sickness." The maximum fine for violation was ten dollars.

Welsh's Café, at the corner of Main and Liberty, would have been an example of a saloon located on a corner to better spot unfriendly Sunday police enforcement, as well as a place likely to have been vulnerable to enforcement of Sunday laws against "billiard rooms… patronized by disorderly or disreputable characters." *From the collection of the Public Library of Cincinnati and Hamilton County.*

In addition to selling alcohol on Sundays, state law in 1831 also prohibited "sporting, rioting, quarreling, hunting, fishing, shooting, or [working] at common labor." Violations were punishable by a five-dollar fine. By the later nineteenth century, the wink-and-a-nod reality of the enforcement of Sunday laws was making itself apparent in the laws themselves. The ban on Sunday labor had carved out a number of exceptions that were not in the original statute. The labor prohibition began to exempt "those who conscientiously observe the seventh day of the week as the Sabbath." State law also added provisions that seemed redundant to both the Sunday ban on alcohol sales and the ban on Sunday labor. Anyone who

> *participates in or exhibits to the public with or without charge…any theatrical or dramatic performance of any kind…or any base-ball playing, or any ten-pins or other games of similar kind or kinds, or participates in keeping any low or disorderly house of resort, or shall sell, dispose of, or give away any ale, beer, porter or spirituous liquors in any building appendant and adjacent thereto, where any such show, performance is given…shall…*

be fined in any sum not exceeding one hundred dollars, or be confined in the
county jail not exceeding six months.

Although the various Sunday laws were not written in the alternative, that was essentially how they were enforced. If you lived in a rural, predominantly Anglo-Protestant, native-born town like Hillsborough, the birthplace of the Woman's Christian Temperance Union, the city could choose to entirely prevent the sale of alcohol on Sundays and cause all businesses to be closed. If, on the other hand, you lived in German-filled, sopping wet Cincinnati, you could overlook the prohibition on selling alcohol on Sundays and the Sunday labor law, and when law-and-order citizens created political pressure, you could stage a crackdown on "low or disorderly" establishments, places featuring burlesque shows or other venues particularly abhorrent to the temperance-loving churchgoers.

One such faux law-and-order moment occurred after the April 6, 1878 decree. On the Monday after the weekend following the decree, the

Peoples Theater was one of Over-the-Rhine's notoriously lowbrow theatres, featuring entertainment like Wild West shows and burlesque. The copula is gone, but the front building of the theatre complex remains on the northwest corner of Thirteenth and Vine. The main theatre hall pictured behind the corner building has been razed and is a surface parking lot. Sister theatres Heuck's and the Standard (aka Vine Street Opera House) have both been demolished. *From the collection of the Public Library of Cincinnati and Hamilton County.*

Cincinnati Commercial Gazette reported that a "billiard saloon proprietor, named David Billinghiemer, who has an establishment over the Rhine, was arrested yesterday and taken, together with thirteen men who were playing in the place, to the Bremen Street Station-house." (Bremen Street is now Republic.) A theatre owner on Vine Street was arrested, as were the owner of the Atlantic Garden on Vine Street and his assistant. The owner and a waiter at "a billiard saloon [that] was found in full blast" rounded out the arrests. These nineteen men may have been the unlucky examples because they failed to adequately lubricate their local beat cop, irritated the wrong person in city government, were particularly raucous at the wrong moment or just lost a random lottery, but it seems safe to assume that thousands of equally blatant violations of the police chief's decree were occurring throughout the city on the same day. These nineteen men were an example of Cincinnati's commitment to law and order—as long as it was just temporary and just for political theatre. The following weeks of crime coverage are notably absent any arrests for violations of Sunday laws. In fact, the pages of the *Cincinnati Commercial Gazette* display a tremendous irony the following week.

Although never attaining the same popularity or longevity as "Porkopolis," Cincinnati was also nicknamed "the Paris of America." The title gained some popular use in the late 1800s and was utilized by travel guides and other civic booster materials to emphasize the city's sophistication and renowned festive spirit. The phrase was first coined by an editorial note in a Monday edition of the *Cincinnati Commercial Gazette* celebrating all of the beer-soaked festivities that occurred on the previous day: Easter Sunday— just two weeks after the city's alleged crackdown on Sunday law violations. Due to an unusual burst of warm weather that precluded the need to burn coal for heat, the editorial noted that "there was no canopy of smoke over the scene [from the hilltops] to obscure any of the glories of the Paris of America." "Sunday in the Paris of America" never specifically mentions Over-the-Rhine or alcohol consumption, but it does celebrate the fact that "the greater portion of the immense population in the lower levels of the city were out," as well as the festive atmosphere in the hilltop resorts' "beer and wine gardens." The entertainment in these places included music and various displays and attractions, but it came primarily from a beer mug. (This would have been particularly true of the resort on "Price's Hill," where "no music was offered.") And while the focus is placed on the hilltops, the "glories of the Paris of America" viewed from the vantage point of the Highland House, Lookout House and Bellevue House would have been primarily Over-the-Rhine.

The same issue of the *Gazette* also raves about an Easter Day clothing sale in a downtown retail store. Of course, the employees in this store, the wait staff and musicians, as well as the carriage drivers, streetcar and incline plane operators who transported people to these places, were all violating the Sunday labor law, and everyone serving beer or other alcoholic beverages was violating that Sunday liquor law as well. The celebration of all the activity occurring on a Sunday—Easter Sunday at that—just two weeks after the decree to enforce the Sunday laws was published in the same newspaper appears ironic, but it illustrates a nuanced and unwritten code. You could do what you wanted in Cincinnati on Sundays as long as you weren't too obnoxious about it. Occasionally, somebody would need to get arrested for appearances, but taking care of your local beat cop would minimize your chances of being that unlucky business owner.

In the wink-and-a-nod political climate of 1879, a saloon owner ran a campaign for city councilman of the Eighteenth Ward. George Barnesdale Cox came from modest means. He was born to British immigrants, and his father died when he was only eight. Cox worked various jobs, including deliveryman, bartender, newsboy and lookout for gambling establishments, until he had worked his way up to co-owning his own saloon on the corner of Longworth and John Streets. (Today, this would be roughly where the convention center is located.) Cox's primary motivation for running for council was to get the power to stop the police from hassling his saloon, a place described as "the common sort, which combined with the sale of liquor various gambling games." The Eighteenth Ward ran from Third Street to Seventh, bounded on its east side by Race Street and on its west side by streets that no longer exist. The ward was a uniquely mixed part of the city: the eastern side of it contained affluent residents and the western side contained an African American section and a red-light district. Benefiting from friendships and connections he had made in years of serving the public drinks, Cox won the election. He served two terms. George Cox would never run for or hold elected office again. Instead, he would become a wildly successful political operative that caused him to be called "dictator," "King of Cincinnati" and, most commonly, "Boss Cox."

Before becoming one of the most powerful political operatives in the nation, "Boss" Cox was motivated to run for city council in order to stop the police from interfering with business at his saloon. *From the collection of the Public Library of Cincinnati and Hamilton County.*

At the time Cox was elected, his Republican Party was in a minority position in Cincinnati. That was about to change. Ironically, the victories of immigrant Democrats in the 1850s and the decades following, coupled with an outrage over political corruption, was about to lead to a Republican takeover of city government and an era of machine politics that would become notorious for its corruption. It would not have been possible without the help of Over-the-Rhine.

Cox built a political machine that was eventually said to be "more compact and closely knit than any of the political machines which have dominated New York, Philadelphia, Chicago, St. Louis or San Francisco." Cox was described as "more autocrat" than New York's infamous Boss Tweed "ever dreamed of being." This political power was derived in a manner that would be almost impossible today. He surrounded himself with a close group of social-political acquaintances who became "the gang." Although eventually vilified, Cox and his top lieutenants were generally well liked. "Surrounded by a motley crowd of former boxers and baseball players, newspaper reporters, vaudeville and burlesque performers, and other Vine Street characters," Cox's men conducted business nightly in Over-the-Rhine saloons, commonly found at their own table in Wielert's beer garden. Wielert's even cut a hole in the back fence of the beer garden so that Cox wouldn't have to walk around the block to get to Republican conventions that were commonly held at Central Turner Hall, which backed up to Wielert's beer garden.

Many of Cox's trusted associates and entourage were German, including August (Garry) Herrmann, a lifelong Over-the-Rhine resident who would become one of Cox's most valuable associates. Herrmann had a number of skills. He was excellent with numbers, said to be capable of carrying the city's budget around in his head. He was also liked by the press and was considered to be a great public relations man—and he could drink. Herrmann had a reputation for starting his evenings in Over-the-Rhine, drinking until about midnight and then moving to meet a "more exclusive set of drinkers" downtown. Often up until 4:00 a.m., he was also known for arriving at the office punctually every morning.

Above: Doug Bootes, Mike Bootes, Amy Morgan, Steve Hampton, Mark Mahoney and Greg Hardman stand in the background watching a backhoe tear away the sidewalk in search of underground rooms.

Right: After numerous backhoe loads of debris were removed, a room was discovered and excavated next to Mike Bootes's basement.

The entrance to the tunnel under McMicken as it appears from the subbasement lagering cellars. The steel beam header above the tunnel entrance indicates that it was added long after the lagering cellar was put into use. Following Prohibition, lagering cellars were sealed off and the ventilation shafts on the walls and ceilings were used as garbage chutes. Over decades, almost entire subbasement chambers have become filled with coal ash and rubbish and the stone floors have developed layers of mud from porous walls, but when they were in use, these tunnels were kept immaculate and hygienic—probably some of the cleanest places in nineteenth-century Over-the-Rhine.

The brew house of the Kauffman Brewery as it appears today at 1622 Vine Street.

Above: One of three large lagering tunnels comprising roughly eleven thousand square feet that was found sealed off under the basement of the former Kauffman Brewery.

Opposite bottom: The tunnel as it appeared when the north side ended in a pile of rubble. It is barely large enough to permit a person to fit through it and was likely used to transport beer from the brew house to bottling facilities through pipes.

Above: Tunnel going under Hamer Street and connecting subterranean portions of the Kauffman Brewery. Unlike the small tunnel that connected sections of Crown, the Kauffman tunnel would have been large enough to permit the transfer of barreled beer and raw materials.

Left: Hops are carved into the stone detail on the Kauffman brewery building on Vine Street.

Above: The six-point brewers' star, a symbol of beer purity, as it appears on the 1886 Sohn Brewery building on McMicken (aka the Mohawk or Clyffside Brewery).

Right: Decorative, intricate iron- and steelwork was common inside the breweries that flourished in the later half of the nineteenth century. Identical examples of this beer barrel stair post, as it appears today inside the Sohn Brewery building, can be seen in numerous historic interior photos of different breweries.

Bellevue Incline Plane, Cincinnati, Ohio.

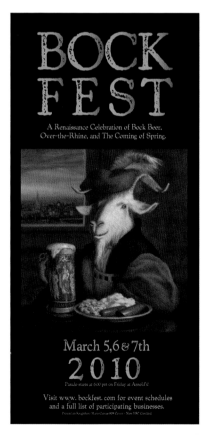

BOCK
FEST

A Renaissance Celebration of Bock Beer,
Over-the-Rhine, and The Coming of Spring.

March 5, 6 & 7th
2010

Parade starts at 6:00 pm on Friday at Arnold's!

Visit www.bockfest.com for event schedules
and a full list of participating businesses.

Above: This turn-of-the-century postcard shows the journey up to the Bellevue House. It illustrates the contrast between the dark, dismal, smoke-filled environment of Over-the-Rhine and the green, pastoral setting and fresh air that awaited at the end of this journey to Clifton Heights. *From the collection of the Public Library of Cincinnati and Hamilton County.*

Left: *Courtesy of artist Jim Effler and Mike Keidel, Bockfest art cocreator and lead designer.*

Opposite bottom: A sneak peek into the lagering tunnels beneath the new Hudepohl-Schoenling Brewery. Currently, these lagering cellars can only be accessed by entering the subbasement of the building across the street, following a tunnel under Hamer Street and crawling through a hole. Future plans will make them accessible for tours through the brewery.

Originally part of the Kauffman Brewery complex, and used for decades after Prohibition by the Husman Potato Chip company, this building on Hamer Street is becoming the new office and future home of production facilities for the Christian Moerlein, Burger, Little Kings and Hudepohl-Schoenling brands.

Left: A cherub carved into the Sohn Brewery raises a glass of overflowing beer on the most ornamental of Over-the-Rhine's remaining brewery buildings.

Below: America's first large-scale music hall was dedicated during the May Festival of 1878. Home to the Cincinnati Symphony Orchestra and the Cincinnati Opera, it has housed a wide range of events, including the Democratic National Convention in 1880 and, more dubiously, the public meeting on March 28, 1884, that led to the courthouse riots.

At the time Cox won his first council election, the city was entering a decade characterized by violence, turmoil and corruption. Both the court system and the police department were flagrantly corrupt. Joseph Foraker, governor, senator and on-and-off Cox ally, characterized city elections as "attended by frauds, committed in the interest of Democrats, by a gang of unscrupulous scoundrels who" stuffed ballot boxes and doctored returns. As a result, "every election day was a day of disorder, violence, and more or less of rioting and bloodshed." In 1885, Cincinnati voted for a change and entered a long period of Republican rule.

The Republicans did bring change, and a lot of it was positive. The police force was de-politicized. Officers were hired by a nonpartisan board of police commissioners appointed by the governor. Once hired, officers underwent extensive training for the first time. The park

Over-the-Rhine native August Herrmann was one of the most critical members of "Boss" Cox's inner circle. His skills included public relations, a near photographic memory of the city budget and a remarkable capacity for drink. *From the collection of the Public Library of Cincinnati and Hamilton County.*

system was expanded. A new city hall was constructed. Clifton, Avondale and Westwood were annexed, building the city's tax base. Certain types of graft and inefficiency were eliminated, and under the direction of Cox, "business methods" made the city more efficient; but these methods came with their own forms of corruption.

Cox controlled the Republican Party. Under his administration, party conventions became formalities. The Cox slate sailed through nominations. In fact, Cox was even rumored to be able to influence Democratic primaries to ensure that a weak candidate would get put forward. "Cox Democrats" aided the Boss in exchange for their share of political appointments and graft. Operations were run tightly, and a network of Cox informants made sure that ward bosses toed the line and kept tight lips. Of course, all of this ran on money and payoffs.

Disputes over control of rail lines and gas and electric utility systems dominated most of the early Cox era. These disputes were resolved effectively but not necessarily in the best interest of the city. August

Herrmann was appointed to chair an administrative board that helped push the city's legislative agenda and dole out city contracts. Not surprisingly, this board played an instrumental role in giving street-paving monopolies to Cox associates. After General Hickenlooper entered a three-year contract with Cox for "services," Herrmann's board helped Hickenlooper's Cincinnati Gas, Light and Coke Company maintain a monopoly over city services. Hickenlooper's company remained in city hall's favor until sometime after Cox went off the payroll. Edison Power and Light cut into Hickenlooper's territory in a deal that earned Cox and Herrmann an estimated $12,000 in bribes. (The estimate came from Hickenlooper, whose personal experiences apparently made him familiar with the fee schedule for bribery.) Difficult questions surrounding the ownership and operation of rail services received similarly expedient resolution: Consolidated Traction Company, represented by Cox ally Joseph Foraker, received a fifty-five-year lease with very favorable terms.

Other perks were more crude. Cox's pick for police court clerk had his own "business method" for handling enforcement of Sunday closing laws. He arrested actors and baseball park employees for working on Sunday, collected bail and released them without trial because it was impossible to get convictions on the charges. In some cases, he demonstrated his courtesy and refrained from interrupting performances by collecting "fines" in advance of scheduled events. This brought the civil official a supplemental income of between $150 and $200 a week. As irritating as this may have been to those paying the bribes, it was all just part of the cost of doing business on Sundays.

The police court clerk was not alone in his system for supplemental income. The city's new professional police force also worked out their own payment schedules. In exchange for free food and booze, the local beat cop would look the other way when passing a saloon open on Sundays. There were some professional courtesies and some occasional flaws in the system. In respect for the officers and to play along with the pantomime that they were enforcing the law, front entrances of saloons were often closed on Sundays, and customers had to come through a door in the side or the rear (easily accommodated in Over-the-Rhine, where grocer's alleys provide a street-front entrance to a side corridor). It also became a common practice to reverse the weekday trend of giving away a free lunch with the purchase of beer and give away beer on Sunday with the purchase of lunch (thereby not selling it on Sunday). Sometimes the system had hiccups. Whether due to pressure from superiors, a personal beef, a power trip or the motivation to up his supplemental income, a beat cop would occasionally go rogue and bust a joint for Sunday law violations. The best insurance against this fate was to own a saloon on a corner. This real estate was coveted both because it was visible to potential customers from multiple angles and because lookouts for the bar could also see cops coming from any direction.

There were hassles and annoyances, but those who made a living selling alcoholic beverages were pretty comfortable with the unofficial customs and practices that let them operate on Sundays. In fact, the large hilltop resorts, the zoo, the Redstockings' games and the more reputable theatres seem to have been relatively free from harassment beyond the advance "fines" paid to the police court clerk. Political pressure started to threaten this comfortable system and led to a showdown in 1889 that became known as the "Saloonkeepers' Rebellion."

Growing statewide temperance sentiment caused the Ohio legislature to pass new legislation during Cincinnati native Joseph Foraker's first term as governor that raised the stakes on the wink-and-a-nod tradition of ignoring Sunday laws in Cincinnati. The changes in the law, in part, made penalties much more severe. The law now imposed a fine of "not more than $100 nor less than $50" and jail time of "not more than thirty nor less than ten days." Far more importantly, upon conviction of violation, "the place where such liquor is sold" was to be declared "a common nuisance," and the court was required to "order [it] shut up" unless the owner could post a $1,000 bond. Every establishment selling alcohol also had to pay an annual $250 fee, and failure to pay the fee would result in a lien on the premises.

Governor Joseph Foraker and Boss Cox had their squabbles, but Foraker was generally a Cox man. He owed his success partly to Cox's political machine, a force that had extended its power well beyond Cincinnati's borders but that still ran business over steins of beer in Over-the-Rhine. Cox kept power, in part, by making sure that the "drys" didn't get a foothold in Cincinnati. Foraker clearly new that, but he also saw an increasing number of Ohio voters, particularly in rural areas, becoming more aggressive about temperance reforms or state prohibition. The liquor question had rising importance, and a candidate's stand could make or break an election. When Foraker was first elected governor on January 11, 1886, he said in an inaugural speech:

The question that largely engaged the attention of the people was what should be done with respect to the liquor traffic. This question is of the greatest importance, but it is so related to personal habits and private morals as to render it impossible to make it a political question in the ordinary sense...The evils of this business are of such character that good men of all parties should stand together for their suppression, and it is thought the time has at last come when they may do so...There should be, therefore, an immediate enactment of efficient measures to prevent and suppress the evils of intemperance, including the imposition of a tax upon the business wherever carried on.

The $250 tax and the increased penalties were the result. This was a calculated move. Liquor licenses (sometimes couched as a "tax" for state constitutional reasons) were hated by both extremes of the liquor question. Prohibitionists thought that the demon alcohol should be illegal—period. Taxing it legitimized it. Saloon owners, on the other hand, simply didn't want to pay it. It was a significant amount of money at the time, and a lot of the city's saloons were small places. The position let Foraker walk a line. He could look tough on the excesses of the saloon trade but also help ensure its continued existence by making it an important source of state revenue.

Taxes helped keep alcohol production and sales legal, but they also put small operators out of business. More importantly, at a time when the average lower middle-class German worked six days a week, Sunday was often a saloon, beer garden or resort's most important day of the week. The occasional bribe was life, but taking Sunday closing laws seriously was a threat to the livelihoods of thousands of Cincinnatians. However, while running for reelection in 1889, Foraker pushed for just that. He wrote an open letter to Cincinnati mayor Mosby encouraging him to enforce the beefed-up laws and shut down Sunday business.

A meeting of somewhere between five hundred and one thousand saloon owners (accounts vary) was held at Central Turner Hall in Over-the-Rhine to protest the stricter laws and Foraker's call to enforce them. Several prominent saloon owners, including Louis Mecklenberg of Mecklenberg Gardens, ran the meeting that ended in the cheering and virtually unanimous adoption of a series of resolutions:

Meyer Brothers Café at 1319 Vine Street would have been typical of Over-the-Rhine saloons. The long, narrow floor plan, wood floors and tin ceiling are common of what remains of the neighborhood's storefronts. *Courtesy of the Cincinnati Historical Society Library, Cincinnati Museum Center.*

WHEREAS, the well-known Owen law, through which corruption and hypocrisy can sneak in everywhere, threatens to become established in Cincinnati, and

WHEREAS, no concerted action has been taken to resent the said Law, which is an insult to common sense; therefore, be it

Resolved, *that we, the saloon-keepers here assembled, openly oppose this law, which is unpopular and damaging to our business; and, therefore, we have decided to keep our places of business quietly open on Sunday, and all succeeding Sundays, conducting our business as on any other day, and avoiding all disturbances.*

Resolved, *that we condemn the side and back door business as corrupting in its tendency, and will make it our special duty to oppose it by all means.*

Resolved, *that each saloon-keeper who signs the resolution of this meeting shall have our solid protection in every case of prosecution, and the expense thereof shall be defrayed by our own means.*

Hundreds of owners signed an oath that said that they would pledge "by our word of honor" to keep their front doors open on Sundays. In fact, they further agreed to use their best efforts "to prevent all business by those who keep only their back and side doors open" and appointed representatives for different wards to call these businesses to the attention of the police. The saloon owners were instructed to get bondsmen, and the committee assumed the duty to make sure that the police court clerk was ready "at all time" to issue bonds. A "first class lawyer" was hired. The July 25 meeting adjourned after a final motion was passed that called for all those arrested on Sunday to "meet at Turner hall [on] Monday morning and march in a body to the police station, with music." It was Henry David Thoreau–style civil disobedience, but it backfired.

On July 26, 1889, a civic organization called the Committee of Five Hundred that included prominent citizens and was organized to push for law and order held a meeting where members "debated the Sunday closing question in secret" but made sure that the *Cincinnati Evening Post* published a small article the same day noting their conclusion that Mayor Mosby was "scored as being in sympathy with the saloonists." Of course, this was basically true. Actual enforcement of Sunday laws would have been political suicide in Cincinnati, and substantively supporting temperance or prohibition causes was out of the question; but it was also a problem with a large and growing number of voters to appear too cozy with purveyors of debauchery and drunkenness. After all, the Republicans had come to power in both the city and the state promising to fight corruption and bring order.

Even a significant number of fellow saloon owners saw the folly in the strategy of forcing city government into a position that required it to either openly announce tolerance of violations of the law or engage in actual enforcement of it. The president of the official Saloonkeepers Association went fishing on Sunday and clarified that his organization had nothing to do with the rebellion. A fellow saloonist commented: "Those men are a set of fools," saying that the participants were "owned by the brewers" and being used by them as pawns. He also predicted that their actions would force stricter enforcement and higher license fees regardless of who won the next elections. His judgment was far better than the participants of the rebellion.

The strategy not only backfired, it backfired splendidly and in unforeseen ways. The meeting of saloon owners was a citywide call, but it further polarized reaction to saloons and alcohol on ethnic and partly geographic lines. A majority of organizers appear to have owned saloons in Over-the-Rhine, with the remainder from heavily German areas like Cumminsville and Corryville, and the meeting was conducted in German. Judge Ermston, who would preside over anyone arrested in the Saloonkeepers' Rebellion, displayed his bias in advance: "I notice most of the law-defying saloonists are foreigners or of foreign birth. Americans have too much respect for themselves to destroy the laws." The organizers of the Saloonkeepers' Rebellion, a body that called itself the League for the Preservation of Citizens' Rights, also had a difficult time getting participation from the saloon owners south of the Rhine. The rebellion was becoming more focused on Germans and on Over-the-Rhine, and it was drawing broad attention in unwanted ways.

The saloon owners had valid complaints. The wink-and-a-nod system did, in fact, breed corruption and undermine respect for the law (in ways that would be drastically magnified during Prohibition). In addition to all of their other resolutions, the saloon owners had made the demand that *all* violations of the Sunday labor law be enforced. This was intended to show the hypocritical manner in which the law was applied. Although the prohibition against "common labor" made it illegal for anyone to engage in his or her ordinary vocation on Sunday, it was almost exclusively enforced against liquor establishments and theatres.

The saloonists also had precedent and some reason to be optimistic about their success. A similar crackdown resulting from a change in state law had occurred in the spring of 1882. The result was an estimated four hundred saloons remaining open "in full blast all day," resulting in only one prosecution citywide. In subsequent years, when people were arrested, juries refused to convict them. The members of the League for the Preservation of Citizens' Rights lived in a city where coming out for the "drys" was political suicide and where the average citizen loved a cold beer. With the right direction, the group might have become politically influential, illustrating the political advantage of rolling back some of the more stringent laws, but they didn't have the right direction, and they had bad timing. In 1889, the Haymarket riot in Chicago and the courthouse riot were still fresh topics. Regardless of actual culpability, popular belief held that the Haymarket riot in 1886 had been caused by German anarchists, feeding xenophobic rhetoric about the genetic, antidemocratic nature of Germans. And the German working class had played an undeniable role in the courthouse riots of 1884. Some of the city's "better" citizens felt that the morality and safety of the whole city were being threatened by the German working class. None of this was lost on Governor Foraker, who also drew comparisons between the courthouse riot and the Saloonkeepers' Rebellion.

The "rebellion" drew the attention of the state. A bipartisan group of one hundred citizens from Batavia wrote a letter to Mayor Mosby admonishing him that the "people of Ohio rely upon you to sustain the law as against the revolutionists who have openly defied the state and announced their intentions to keep open their saloons on Sunday." The citizens of Batavia also hinted at ethnic division: "Rebellion, under the circumstances, is treason, and treason should be made odious." Governor Foraker agreed. He wrote in his memoirs: "We had had enough experience in Cincinnati in connection with the burning of our Court House and the mob-rule and the rioting that followed to cause me to feel that there was no safety against such dangers except by crushing such outbreaks in their incipiency." On July 27, the Cincinnati *Evening Post* reported that "it was rumored this afternoon that Gov. Foraker had advised with Mayor Mosby that the Ohio National Guards would be called on tomorrow if necessary to uphold the law."

An *Evening Post* editorial entitled "A Friendly Word" distinguished between speech and action, noting that no American could be punished for attending a meeting like the one at Turner Hall but that engaging in overt rebellion was a different matter. It also drew a distinction from the standard practice of Sunday sales, which the paper called an "individual act" versus "an advertised conspiracy." The editorial called for peace by asking that the saloon owners who had signed the pledge rethink their position and refrain from forcing a confrontation. Mosby said that he hoped the rebellion was a "bluff" but that the city was prepared to take all necessary action. The chief of police warned: "We will be ready for them."

Mayor Mosby had no option other than a show of force. Possibly concerned that the presence of the National Guard could incite violence, he called for no outside assistance. Instead, he showed confidence that the matter would not get out of control and could be handled by city government. On Sunday, July 28, all of the city's police force was on active duty with backup from the firemen. When Sunday came, considerably fewer than the 1,200 saloon owners who reportedly put their signatures on the resolutions in the days following the Turner Hall meeting seem to have followed through. In fact, one of the key organizers even decided to remain closed and only opened his saloon by the Lion Brewery after he was "compelled to do so by those who attended the meeting." A reported 138 saloon owners participated in the rebellion. The city's police marched over the Vine Street bridge and made the first arrest of a saloon owner, Hans Hoeger, at Thirteenth and Vine at 6:15 a.m. Arrests and small skirmishes occurred throughout the day, primarily in Over-the-Rhine and the area just west of the canal. Several squabbles "nearly precipitated a riot." Angry words were exchanged and some stones were thrown, but no major violence occurred. A total of 164 arrests were made, including several saloon customers and one particularly persistent owner who was arrested three separate times in the course of the day.

On the following Monday, the *Evening Post* wrote that the "overt act of rebellion" had occurred and that now the issue must be "forever decided": "Shall the state of Ohio surrender to the Cincinnati saloonkeepers' rebellion?" The *Post* goaded the court, saying that the "eyes of the people of Cincinnati, of Ohio, of the United States are on the Police court of Cincinnati." The presiding Judge Ermston did not disappoint. He raised minimum bonds to $3,000 for each participant, except for a $5,000 bond for the owner who had been arrested three times. He said that each should be prepared to issue a $10,000 bond for subsequent offenses and instructed the clerk to change the bond process to make it much more difficult to post bond on Sundays. This effectively assured that every arrest would result in some amount of jail time. The revolving-door system had been closed. Violations of the Sunday law would be treated like crimes.

The Saloonkeepers' Association held a meeting a few days later to condemn the owners who participated in the rebellion. Its members passed a resolution stating that the actions of association members who had participated deserved the "severest censure" because their actions "could only strengthen the cause of our opponents." And it did strengthen the cause of their opponents. Members of the Law and Order League were not content with the arrest of the rebellion participants. They spent Sunday July 28 busily taking down notes and names of establishments conducting side-door business with no complaint from the police. Feeling the spoils of a victory that had been essentially handed to them by the saloon owners' poor tactical decisions, the Law and Order League and the Committee of Five Hundred kept the heat up. On Sunday evening, August 14, Mayor Mosby summoned the president of the Redstockings and all of the managers of the theatres to his office to advise them that Sunday games and performances could no longer be permitted. The manager of the ball club asked for leniency to permit the remaining four scheduled Sunday games to be played. The mayor refused, saying that if the team attempted to play on Sunday he would "arrest the manager, every one of the players, the umpire, the bartenders, the ground keepers and everybody connected with the game." It was recognized that theatres "catering to the masses" would be hurt. The manager of Heuck's, a Vine Street theatre meeting this description, realistically conceded that so "long as the public demanded amusement and the authorities did not suppress them by an enforcement of the law it was to our advantage to give them," but he resigned himself to the necessity of closure if the law was actually going to be enforced.

On the following Sunday, the ballpark was silent. The theatres were closed. Saloons doing business did it discreetly. Enforcement continued, but "only four or five arrests were made" "for violation of the Sunday law and common labor law" on Sunday, August 19. On the following Monday, the Post reported: "Only 17 drunks on the Police court docket yesterday morning…for a city of about 300,000 inhabitants. Surely the faithful execution of the laws seven days of the week is giving Cincinnati a decrease of domestic misery and a happier and more peaceful life." The Law and Order League and the Committee of Five Hundred were equally jubilant. They wrote a joint letter to Mosby to congratulate him "on the efficient performance of [his] duty in the enforcement of our Sunday Laws." The letter hints at greater things for Mosby if he continued to toe the line: "We think that we can assure you that the great majority of our citizens in Cincinnati, and a still greater majority of them in the State; will be much pleased with your course [of action], and a continuance in it will not only secure their hearty approval, but will do much to popularize the Republican party which has already honored you, and which will doubtless honor you still more in the future."

The Cincinnati Saloonkeepers' Rebellion was over. It ended not just with a whimper but with a loss of ground as well. Doing business on Sundays became more difficult and more risky. A total of 2,907 liquor licenses were granted in 1889, generating $665,669.13 in city revenue. Undoubtedly, the fee a beat cop charged to keep his eyes, ears and mouth shut increased. Open insurrection was not repeated. The German-Americans of Over-the-Rhine shifted all future battles over "personal liberty" (i.e., liquor) to the political system.

Over-the-Rhine played a significant role in the Boss Cox years. In some ways, the wards in Over-the-Rhine and its adjacent German districts (e.g., Mohawk-Brighton and parts of the West End) typified and justified nativist objections to immigrants. Nativists accused immigrants of creating or at least enabling political machines by voting out of ignorance or shortsightedness or selling votes for a drink or small amounts of money. The allegation had merit. Poor urban neighborhoods were susceptible to all kinds of graft and collusion. Wagons would bring voters in from other wards without even the pretense of concealing that they were literally being trucked in to stuff ballots, and corrupt poll judges looked the other way. Democratic mayor Hunt said that he was inspired to enter city politics when he and a fellow law student spent an election day watching Cox's machine pay African Americans two dollars per vote. Trusted Cox ally and Irish-American ward boss Mike Mullen consistently brought the Irish vote to Cox candidates,[5] and August Herrmann could usually be counted on to do the same with Germans in Over-the-Rhine. However, Over-the-Rhine was distinguishable. It could and did swing its vote on substantive grounds—specifically, a candidate's position on personal liberty.

The first significant challenge to Cox's rule came in 1897. Ironically, it came largely from the hilltop suburbs that had been annexed by Cox man Mayor Caldwell. Although these areas traditionally voted Republican, they resented a political system that used the concentrated numbers of inner-city votes to maintain a virtual dictatorship. Reform Republicans and Democrats came together on a fusion ticket and backed a German-born mayoral candidate named Tafel. The additional votes on the hilltops and the emergence of the fusion strategy made Over-the-Rhine a critical battleground. The *Volksfreund* (the German-language Democratic paper) endorsed him with the promise

5. Mike Mullen was one of the city's most fabled political players, firmly controlling the Irish wards on the lower east side and near the river. While he was "serving" as the inspector of police, Mullen was sentenced to serve a year in jail for rounding up all the African Americans in a ward and locking them up on Election Day to prevent them from voting in 1885.

that the city would "in every respect feel just as 'gemuthlich' as in Germany" if he won. He did.

Although Over-the-Rhine had helped give Cox his power, it did not do so blindly. As the Republican Party became less reliable defenders of personal liberty, party allegiance and allegiance to Cox started to subside. Democrats recognized the importance of the German-American vote in 1906. Supporters of Democratic mayoral candidate Dempsey gave campaign speeches in German in front of German societies. They assured residents of Over-the-Rhine that neither Dempsey nor the temperance-inclined gubernatorial candidate would support prohibition laws. A Dempsey supporter spoke in German at German Day festivities to dissuade fears of nativism in the Democratic Party. He asked and answered: "Do the Germans who live here and the descendants who follow become good American citizens? The answer is emphatically yes." The strategy worked. Reliable Republican wards in Over-the-Rhine and Mohawk-Brighton went Democrat and helped put Dempsey over the top. Cox announced his retirement from politics for the second time. As mayor, Dempsey attempted to implement a Sunday closing policy that "guarantees every one his liberty, and at the same time insures the outward decorum and respect due to the church-going people of the city."

Although he was essentially announcing a comfortable and assured return to the wink-and-a-nod side-door Sunday policy, Dempsey's announcement that he was going to enforce Sunday laws in any manner at all led to an outcry within the city's German societies, the German Day Association being one of them. This society existed primarily to organize an annual German Day on the first Sunday in September. The festival had to be on Sunday because a large number of its attendees worked on Saturdays. The beer sold on this particular Sunday event constituted the Day Association's largest fundraiser, and actual enforcement of Sunday laws threatened its existence. When the group's president announced that it did not have time or resources devoted to battling with the temperance movement, incensed members formed a committee to organize a large protest rally against Sunday enforcement. The rally never happened. The committee concluded that "we have in Mr. Dempsey a mayor so tolerant and liberal and such a friend of personal liberty that we can put all our trust in him." The consensus of the committee was that Dempsey's rhetoric was just another political show for the city's Anglo-Protestant voters, and the Germans were afraid that a rally against Dempsey could damage relations with a friendly candidate—possibly produce the same kind of kickback felt from the Saloonkeepers' Rebellion years before. The committee settled on drafting and circulating a petition to show support for Mayor Dempsey's "liberal" (i.e., lax) enforcement of Sunday laws. In other words, they got a bunch of people to sign a letter thanking the mayor for ignoring the law.

A similar pro-German political strategy worked for Democratic candidate Henry Hunt in 1911. He assured German voters that he would not enforce Sunday closing laws and promised to end corruption and boss rule. Over-the-Rhine and Mohawk-Brighton voted for Hunt and delivered the swing votes necessary to put him in office. As mayor, Hunt kept his promise not to enforce Sunday closing laws but engaged in a morality campaign that targeted saloon "sitting rooms" for women. Not permitted in most of the male-dominated bars themselves, many saloons had separate rooms where men and women could meet together. Sometimes these were respectable places; often they were the part of the saloon where the prostitutes worked. Hunt also sent undercover detectives into German social events looking for immoral behavior. This resulted in temporary revocation of the liquor license at Central Turner Hall for having a dance where "girls in short dresses were being served drinks." Hassling saloons and spying on German society events was taken as an affront on personal liberty, and the German-American wards that helped make Hunt mayor played a pivotal role in defeating his bid for reelection.

Over-the-Rhine and its adjoining German wards had become the key to winning city elections. Cincinnati's German-Americans played a role in elections that was distinguishable from other urban immigrant groups in the machine era of politics—even distinguishable in Cincinnati. In 1911, the Irish and African American wards were all that was left of the reliably Republican voting blocks. You needed Over-the-Rhine to win, and Over-the-Rhine had become a single-issue voting bloc. For a period before World War I, the "wettest" and the most German candidates won. The neighborhood only stuck with Boss Cox when his candidates suited the interests of Over-the-Rhine. A candidate's opinion about a cold beer on a Sunday afternoon was as good an indicator of his electability in Cincinnati as a candidate's position on gay marriage is in Utah today.

For a while, Cox was boss but beer was king in Cincinnati politics. Both would go down for the count in the upcoming years. Cox's city treasurer maintained a "tradition" of personally pocketing the interest earned on city money in private banks. Cox denied ever taking any of these funds, but his denial became the basis for a perjury trial five years later when it was alleged that Cox had received at least $65,000 of the money. An Honest Election Committee chaired by James N. Gamble and charged with exploring the corruption of the Cox years "claimed to possess information, gathered from credible sources, of widespread election frauds, including false registration, illegal voting, and tampering with the count and returns." The 1911 winter–spring session of the Hamilton County grand jury lasted forty-five days, examined over 1,000 witnesses and indicted 123 people associated with Cox's political machine. An equally crushing series of events would castrate the political importance of Over-the-Rhine just a few years later.

AMERICA WINS

When violent Know-Nothing hordes stampeded over the canal, stabbed a brewer to death in the street and unleashed three days of ethnically charged bloodshed in 1855, Over-the-Rhine coalesced as if it were the separate nation that the Know-Nothings saw it to be. It bore the hallmarks of a foreign nation, not just because most of its people spoke a foreign language but also because it was essentially a self-contained society. Its residents came from a wide variety of socioeconomic classes and backgrounds. It had strong leaders who had been brought to Cincinnati by oppression and rebellion in Germanic states in the 1830s and '40s. Like most nineteenth- and early twentieth-century immigrant neighborhoods, Over-the-Rhine residents were drawn together by a common language, food and culture, and they were drawn by joining friends and family members who had come before them. Unlike the waves of immigration that would come in the late nineteenth and early twentieth centuries, they were not entirely defined by poverty. Over-the-Rhine contained some of the best and brightest of its generation and culture; but by the time Cincinnati brewing reached its pinnacle in the 1880s, this had changed.

Significant immigration to Cincinnati's hilltops started in the 1870s, when it started to become feasible. In 1850, there was one omnibus that took residents of Mount Auburn back and forth from downtown, and the journey took *two hours*. The construction of an incline in 1872 made the journey much quicker, and an incline rail line followed in Price Hill in 1875, up to Clifton Heights in 1876, to Mount Adams in 1877 and to Fairview in 1894. Commuting to work downtown from a hilltop home became realistic.

Successful Germans who could afford to leave Over-the-Rhine and its surrounding German neighborhoods started to leave in increasing numbers, and for good reason. Although undoubtedly exciting and vibrant, and still described as a place that maintained a middle-class sense of dignity, life would have been pretty unpleasant in Over-the-Rhine by the late 1800s. The neighborhood became one of the most densely populated places in America in a very short period of time, and this growth occurred in an era without things that we take for granted today: building codes, zoning or pollution regulations. Imagine that you lived on the third floor of 261 West McMicken Avenue, just an ordinary tenement house in Over-the-Rhine. In the late 1800s, the city averaged nearly nine people per dwelling unit. Over-the-Rhine's numbers were typically higher than average, and entire units could be smaller than a Manhattan hotel room or a large master bath in a West Chester McMansion. A bottling works was immediately behind your crowded building. A carpenter was behind the bottle shop, and his business had a slaughterhouse two doors down, adjacent to an ice plant. To your immediate right there was another overcrowded tenement building with a lumber warehouse on the first floor. Twenty feet from it was a saloon that was adjacent to the stables used by the brewery across the street. To your immediate left there was a saloon with a cooperage behind it and a laundry business beside it. Looking immediately across the street you saw a cabinetmaker and a tin shop, next to another saloon. If you didn't like either the saloon to your left, right or across the street, you were in luck because there was also one behind the saloon across the street that had a reputation for prostitution. If none of those quenched your thirst, there was another saloon eight doors west of the one to your left. That saloon had a saloon across the street from it and two more around the corner; but you might want to watch how much you drank in the second one around the corner, because you wouldn't want to get drunk and fall into the adjacent canal that had essentially become an open sewer. Within five hundred feet of your cramped hovel, there was also a shoe factory, a tannery, a hay and grain facility, a wagon shop, a foundry, a buggy manufacturer, a place curing animal hides, a second brewery, at least three more saloons and thousands of people all living on top of one another in buildings with no yards.

Over-the-Rhine tenement buildings lacked more than yards. They were built before the extensive manufacture of plumbing materials. Aside from relying on communal outhouses in cramped courtyards, creative plumbing

The canal as it appeared shortly before its drainage, showing both a complete absence of boat commerce as well as dark, debris-filled water. Depictions from earlier days show women and children floating down the canal on an afternoon outing, but by the time this photo was taken, it was most often described with words like "black" and "malodorous." *From the collection of the Public Library of Cincinnati and Hamilton County.*

solutions included things like running cold water to sinks made out of sheet metal boxes and fastened to the outside of windowsills. There were a handful of very nice family homes in the neighborhood, but even if you could afford one you still had to walk through incredibly congested and filthy streets. A turn-of-the-century account says that merchants and residents swept dirt onto sidewalks and dumped garbage in the streets. Pedestrians had to "step over or wade through slimy water which is run off roofs, from washtubs and yards…into the gutter. On a warm day the stench in some places would knock a horse down." A child of privilege of the time described downtown Cincinnati as "frighteningly ugly and hideously dirty." "We thought life was dirty and smelt bad and had to be washed off you several times a day." Life downtown "meant factories spewing out smoke and stinks, the grimy, endless vistas of warehouses and little shops, the clang and screech of trolley cars, the clatter of horse-drawn beer wagons over cobblestone, the ponderous rush of fire engines, smoke pouring thick from its shiny funnel, its bell clanging and clanging, and the great white horses galloping heavily."

By contrast, the hilltop communities of Clifton, Corryville, Mount Auburn, Walnut Hills, Price Hill and Western Hills were each a fresh, clean oasis. Brewer Christian Moerlein is a great example of the migration of successful German immigrants. Christian Moerlein left Truppach, Bavaria, to come to America and become a brewer in 1841. He left home with the equivalent of forty dollars. He had to walk three hundred miles just to board a ship where he spent almost two months at sea. When he arrived in America, he was down to twelve dollars. Moerlein had a weak grasp of the language and no job prospects. He failed to find employment in Pittsburgh, kept moving west and arrived in Wheeling, West Virginia, with one dollar and whatever clothing and modest belongings he was carrying. Moerlein worked as a farmhand long enough to make enough money to get to Portsmouth, Ohio, where he worked in a distillery for a few months and finally made his way to Cincinnati in 1842. In Cincinnati, things did not get immediately better. He dug foundations for fifty cents a day. Moerlein learned English, became a blacksmith, opened his own blacksmith shop and finally brewed his first beer in 1853—twelve miserable years after leaving Bavaria to become an American brewer. Beginnings do not get much more humble than this, and the wealth that Moerlein would obtain in subsequent years must have been unimaginable to him when he first made Over-the-Rhine his home.

For most of the 1850s, Moerlein appears to have lived in a tenement building with his brewery partner, Conrad Windish. The success of the brewery let him build his own home beside it on Elm Street about 1860. Moerlein's business grew substantially and quickly. Germans moving out of Over-the-Rhine in the 1870s followed a common pattern of moving north up the canal or north up Vine, most typically no more than a half-mile from the neighborhood's northern borders. In 1870, having brewed his way from poverty to wealth, Moerlein exemplified this pattern by moving his family to a large, decorative home on the corner of Mulberry and Fox (now Loth), near Vine Street, just slightly north of Over-the-Rhine. It was built in the Italianate style, perched on the north side of the hill and approached by stone stairs. The zero lot lines were gone. The home had a large yard surrounded by a decorative iron fence and a stable house in the rear. As impressive as the house would have been originally, an addition almost doubled its size in subsequent years.

By 1877, Moerlein was brewing over seventy-two thousand barrels of beer a year. The brewery started in the back of a blacksmith shop had become

The Christian Moerlein Family home on Mulberry Street as it appears today.

the largest in the state of Ohio and the fourth largest in the United States. Moerlein moved again in 1882 to an even more elaborate and decorative home on Ohio Avenue in Clifton Heights.

Some brewers chose to remain near their breweries. Gottlieb Muhlhauser never left Liberty Street. John Kauffman stayed on Vine, and John Hauck built a large, elegant home on Dayton Street; but Moerlein was not alone in the brewers making the move to higher ground. By 1880, Gambrinus Stock brewer Christian Boss had left his ample home on Broadway to move to Walnut Hills; and as Louis Hudepohl's brewery became successful, he made a similar move from Spring Street to Cleinview Avenue, also in Walnut Hills.

Moerlein was not abandoning his roots or his fellow Germans by moving to Clifton Heights. By the late 1890s, he was one of the richest men in the city but was still described as "modest, open" and "affable." A contemporary said that "there is no concern, of charitable or general interest, in which Mr. Moerlein isn't the very first one to take significant part." He gave to causes frequently, and often anonymously. However, the days of a geographically concentrated German community in Over-the-Rhine were ending as brewing was reaching its pre-Prohibition zenith in the 1870s and '80s. Not only did German-Americans live throughout the city, but Over-the-Rhine was on the social decline as well.

An 1895 travel guide opined:

> *Over the Rhine—Fifteen or twenty years ago the resident or visitor had no sooner entered the northern districts of the city lying beyond Court street across the canal than he found himself in another atmosphere, in all outward seeming almost in a foreign land. Germans and Americans alike loved to call the region "Over the Rhine." But Rome fell and "Over the Rhine" was not immortal. All or nearly all of the leading characteristics which won for it the appellation have passed away.*

By 1898, a similar guide to the city told the visitor or newcomer that the hilltop communities are Cincinnati's "crowning glory." "Cincinnati works in the valley below, but she lives above." "Here reside the families enriched by the industry of the low, smoky town. Here upon these enchanting hills and in these inviting valleys will finally gather the greater part of the population, leaving the city to the smoke and heat when the labors of the day are done."

Although it was becoming more ethnically diverse, the neighborhood continued to be primarily home to working-class German-Americans. Over-the-Rhine also remained the heart of Cincinnati's German community. In fact, the dispersal of Germans throughout the city made the neighborhood more important because it was the place where German-Americans from all over Cincinnati came together. Some German societies found other homes and additional Turner Halls were built, but the majority of societies still kept their halls and meeting locations in Over-the-Rhine, either in one of its German halls or its myriad saloons.

Saloons and beer gardens played an important social role in Over-the-Rhine. Living conditions were cramped and sparse. The saloon acted as a communal living room, a place where men both conducted business and socialized; and the beer gardens were suitable for families and provided a rare opportunity to sit under a tree or a trellis of vines in tightly packed Over-the-Rhine. Many of the Forty-Eighters' generation came to the city with enough money to open saloons. This created bartending jobs for fellow immigrants and helped grow the local brewing business. Saloons also served as welcome centers for new arrivals. A nineteenth-century guide to the city recommends that new arrivals place an ad in the paper describing what type of lodging they are seeking and then "avoid engaging rooms longer than for a week…as the presence of disagreeable people or other contingencies frequently make it desirable to change." Saloons offered a better way. Although motivated primarily by the desire to earn a new regular customer, saloon owners provided a valuable service by often finding new immigrants a place to live and their first job. The newcomer was also likely to be introduced to members of the "Stammtisch." Every decent saloon had a Stammtisch, "a table usually reserved for an informal group of special customers who met customarily once or twice a week to discuss over endless Schoppen of wine or steins of beer the problems of the old and new fatherland." German societies in Over-the-Rhine were said to be as prolific "as the pebbles along the shore of the Ohio." These societies could be singing clubs (Grammer's was home to a singing club composed of bakers), athletic clubs, mutual aid societies or charitable organizations; some were organized for cultural enlightenment and others purely for entertainment. Regardless of their purpose, every self-respecting saloonkeeper wanted to be chosen as a society's "Stammwirt" (host). The reality of Over-the-Rhine saloons was very different from the violent houses of sin, ruin and toil portrayed by the temperance and prohibition movements. Most saloons were reserved exclusively for men. Billiards and bowling lanes were common and looked down upon by better

Grammer's Café. Due largely to the devotion of former owner Jim Tarbell, the bar, bar lights, leaded-glass windows, tin ceiling and hand-cut floor tiles remain intact today. *From the collection of the Public Library of Cincinnati and Hamilton County.*

Wielert's as it appears today.

Wielert's interior dining room as it appeared before Prohibition. *From the collection of the Public Library of Cincinnati and Hamilton County.*

Wielert's Beer Garden.

society, in part, because they often involved wagering. However, saloons were an integral and valuable part of German-American life. Wielert's on Vine is one of the best examples. It served as the unofficial seat of city government, and its house band gave rise to the Cincinnati Symphony Orchestra.

By the late 1800s, the numerous beer gardens that had flourished in Over-the-Rhine in the years following the Civil War started to diminish. Customers preferred to take the incline planes to the hilltop resorts, where the air in the beer gardens did not float by as black particulate dust. Many of the neighborhood's affluent and middle-class citizens were now living on the hills and supporting establishments like Mecklenberg Gardens in Corryville. Over-the-Rhine remained German and it remained vibrant; it just started to get seedier and started becoming a parody of itself. Its once purely authentic German character became a theme for tourists and non-German Cincinnatians. By the end of the nineteenth century, it was Cincinnati's German equivalent of New Orleans's French Quarter.

As it approached the 1900s, the neighborhood "continued to attract out-of-town visitors, suburbanites, politicians, show people, and a motley crowd," but they came for its "contrived German flavor." In the 1880s, the

Located on Vine Street, immediately south of the canal (where the Kroger building now stands), the former Vine Street Opera House had become the Standard Theater, specializing in burlesque by the late 1800s. *From the collection of the Public Library of Cincinnati and Hamilton County.*

neighborhood started to accumulate theatres that Frank Grayson looks back at nostalgically in *Pioneers of Nightlife on Vine* as operating in "bold defiance of all the tenets of morality." The cultural scene that had produced the symphony had become the home of vaudeville and burlesque. The neighborhood had accumulated roughly three hundred saloons within its modern zoning borders, with hundreds more stretching down Central Avenue, west on Liberty and north and south up Vine. These establishments still provided employment, still housed a number of German societies and still served as the communal living rooms for people living in crowded Over-the-Rhine, but the neighborhood was becoming more exclusively working class, and the extraordinary number of saloons in the city was causing a broad spectrum of morality to be exchanged for a higher profit margin. The saloons were becoming a greater liability in a simmering public relations battle.

Changes in the numerous German societies were also helping seal the fate of Over-the-Rhine. Cincinnati's first German mutual aid society was started in 1819. Although it didn't last very long, more substantive groups followed

By 1886, some social changes were reflected in advertisements in the city directory. No longer listed solely by the name of the proprietor, growing competition led to catchy advertising and saw saloons listing ads like "more respectable" businesses; but this increasing competition and visibility was also building backlash against the makers and purveyors of all alcoholic beverages. *From the collection of the Public Library of Cincinnati and Hamilton County.*

as the German population increased. America's first Turnverein society (the Turners), the Germania Lodge and several German singing societies were all founded in 1848 but continued growing in numbers and interests into the late nineteenth century. Groups founded in the 1890s still typically met in Over-the-Rhine even though they were often composed almost entirely of members who lived in other neighborhoods. The organizations had a wide range of missions and purposes, but with the notable exception of the programs created by William Nast's Methodist church on Race Street, they all drank beer—a lot of it. (The Emanuel Center across from Washington Park was originally built for the purpose of keeping young Germans away from alcohol.) Toward the later part of the nineteenth century and the early twentieth, they were also almost entirely composed of the lower middle class. Society officers were often waiters, bartenders, butchers or held similar vocations.

Some organizations, most notably the powerful German Day Association, refused to get involved in political issues, but generally speaking the societies became increasingly unified around two key issues: language and beer. In

1840, Cincinnati's German-American community was primarily responsible for getting state legislation passed that provided funding for German instruction in public schools. By the end of the nineteenth century, this led to extensive bilingual instruction in Cincinnati public schools. Members of the German societies thought it was important to preserve and celebrate their ethnicity, and most believed that keeping a bilingual community was a key to this goal. Therefore, many of the older members were concerned by the fact that the second generation of German-Americans was becoming more assimilated: societies were even starting to hold meetings and keep notes in English. Editorials in the German language press warned that "[a] people's language is its real soul" and "to discard it means to run the danger of losing the most precious essence in a people without being able to absorb the good qualities in another people whose language one has adopted."

The second and more pressing core issue of German-American society life was the political issue of personal liberty. The importance of this principle was expressed by a speaker at a German event in highly philosophical tones: "Let for others moral action consist only in an anxious fulfillment of self-made or blindingly assumed laws, for German moral action is the result of free self-determination whose ultimate authority is the free personality itself. Hence to touch upon the self-determination of the free personality, i.e., the highest good of German being and culture, is to take dead aim at the heart of the German."

In other words, any encroachment on the right to drink beer was an assault on the German soul. Some Germans took umbrage with this level of fixation on beer. An 1878 editorial in the *Deutsche Pioneer* questioned the image that German-Americans were creating for themselves:

> *Who is ever to calculate how much respect we have gained with the cultivated American with our incessant harping on the civilizing powers of the "Gambrinus Juice" [i.e., beer]; and in strolling through the German sections of our cities, in what growing proportion will his respect increase when his eyes alight in every single block on at least two, three, and even four artfully painted signs, each displaying an enormous, overflowing, foaming tankard and bearing the legend "Lager Beer"? Must this not force upon him the conviction that the consumption of beer symbolizes for us the highest and most important task in our lives?*

This was clearly a minority viewpoint. Renewed prohibition movements in the 1890s did, in fact, turn beer into the lifeblood of Germandom. It was observed that "the average German's desire to grasp a cooling mug of beer was transformed into the all-consuming struggle for Personal Liberty."

German societies changed more than just their socioeconomic composition and their limited ideological focus. They also changed the way that they spoke about Germany and how they interacted with the rest of the city. Between 1870 and 1890, all of the old Forty-Eighters who once represented the community's leadership passed away. Also around this period of time, broader American society started becoming obsessed with lineage, heredity and the emerging science of genetics. Much of this movement took the form of supreme snobbery among the American aristocracy. The upper class started carving out their own substrata of classism, judging their fellow millionaires on their lineage. The longer your family had been in America, the more Anglo it was, and the longer it had been rich made you better bred and genetically superior to people with less pure histories. T.S. Matthews, the son of a Matthews and a Procter (of the Procter & Gamble Procters), recalled:

> *The Matthewses did in fact consider themselves a cut above the Procters, partly because they thought themselves better bred—their Welsh-English descent being, in their eyes, superior to the Irish-English line of the Procters—but principally for two other snobbish reasons: they had been Americans for nine generations to the Procters' three; and no Matthews, so they said, had ever been "in trade." The Procters, on the other hand, had grown rich by the somehow shameful process of making soap, and also tallow candles to begin with.*

The German-Americans often took swipes from this über snobbery, but prior to World War I they generally fared a lot better than other immigrant groups. The late nineteenth and early twentieth centuries saw significant changes in immigration patterns. Although these macro patterns were not apparent to people at the time, they started noticing a lot more immigrants arriving from poverty-stricken Eastern European countries. Bloodlines and, later, eugenics were used to explain why the older wave of German immigrants was superior to the newer wave of Slavs and Italians—their ancestry was closer to the English. Cincinnati experienced such a significant amount of German immigration in the mid-nineteenth century because it was the largest and most important city in the West: it was an obvious destination. Similarly, it received fewer of the newer ethnic immigrant groups because it no longer held this position of prominence when they started arriving en masse. It did, however, continue to receive German immigrants who were drawn by family, friends and a German-friendly atmosphere. Due to these patterns and because such a significant and respected percentage of the city was German-American, Cincinnati did not see the degree of nativist ethnic conflict that occurred in eastern cities, but it would have been impossible to be a first- or second-generation immigrant during the Victorian era without feeling some sting of ethnic bigotry.

The Forty-Eighters were democratic rebels. Some of them even saw America as the outpost for spreading democracy to Germany and throughout the world. They loved their fatherland, but they were also critical of it; many of them had left it for deeply ideological reasons. This was far less true of the German-American societies meeting in Over-the-Rhine around the turn of the century. Many were second- or third-generation Cincinnatians, and new arrivals came for financial rather than ideological reasons. This generation of German societies was concerned by anti-German sentiment and equally concerned with the reason why they were starting to escape a lot of the vitriol aimed at other immigrant groups: they were assimilating. To many of Cincinnati's German-Americans, this was a good thing; but the people who lived in Over-the-Rhine and the societies that met there were more closely attached to their ethnicity. They viewed the loss of their Germanness as a loss of both identity and moral grounding. Together, these factors made the German societies increasingly more nationalistic. A pattern emerged that would put these societies on the path of self-destruction. The more they perceived assimilation among their peers, the more overtly German they became. The more they saw anti-German sentiment in the community, the more loudly they praised the fatherland. Their celebrations also started taking on more direct imagery of the fatherland and increasingly began incorporating German iconography and military-style marches. There were Cincinnatians who resented this, and it was often derided as "clannish," but it drew little meaningful reaction. Around the turn of the century, Cincinnati's Germans were primarily viewed as an exotic curiosity by the city's non-Germans. They were part of the city's character, not a threat or a problem. Over-the-Rhine passed through the first decade of the twentieth century as the heart of Cincinnati Germandom and as the city's famed and infamous German entertainment district. Then came the Great War.

On August 1, 1914, Cincinnati's German-American community received the news that Germany had declared war on Russia, commencing its involvement in what would become World War I. Although disruption with ship traffic prevented them from making it out of the country, droves of Cincinnati's German community who were not yet citizens reported to the Austrian and Hungarian consulate in Over-the-Rhine, ready to join the German army. Cincinnati's German-born mayor Spiegel announced that "the sympathies of the Americans should be with Germany, not only because of the justice of Germany's cause but also because Germany has always been a better friend to the United States than any other of the contending countries." Phonograph players blared German waltzes out of the windows of Over-the-Rhine apartments, and its beer gardens and saloons filled with people seeking news about the war. "The German community, or at least that part which was wont to gather nightly in Over-the-Rhine, soon settled down around its beer tables to fight the war with all the more gusto."

The rhetoric of the German societies and the German press was ratcheted up in ways that would be regretted in the following years. By genuine coincidence, Ohio had another statewide Prohibition amendment vote on the November 14, 1914 ballot. The *Volksblatt* warned voters: "Just as our brothers and sisters are presently sacrificing goods and chattels, body and soul, across the ocean to save Germandom from its enemies, so must we, with the same readiness for sacrifice, overcome our enemies" (i.e., prohibitionists). The *Freie Presse* rallied voters with similar rhetoric: "We are at war too, at war against hypocrisy, intolerance; and against nativist presumptuousness and moralistic pretentiousness." German societies responded to the *Freie Presse* editorial by marching to its offices interchangeably singing "Die Wacht am Rhein" and "My Country 'Tis of Thee." After the measure was defeated, the *Freie Presse* rejoiced with an equally divisive tone: "The American Allies—Reformers, Grapejuicers, Watersimpletons, Bullmoosers, Suffragettes, etc.—have now learned what the Entente has known for some time: how German blows taste."

The Great War rallied Cincinnati's German-Americans. By the time the war started, the city's German societies had become isolated from the city's successful German-American elite. The German affluent gave to German causes, but they seem to have focused most of this charity on the German orphan asylum, the German old age home and similarly safe and socially respectable causes. The war brought them back into the fold. Over-the-Rhine's residents and lower-middle-class German societies joined the hilltop German affluent in conducting fundraisers for war aid societies to benefit German families and orphans. Decades of squabbling between different societies and religious denominations seemed almost forgotten. Prominent German-Americans, including brewers Moerlein, Lackmann, Windish and Muhlhauser, gave generously to German aid societies. The German press, in decline before the war, saw a spike in sales. Attendance to the German theatre increased.

In the first couple years of the war, the German-language press was merciless against President Wilson's "Anglomania" and glowing in its certainty of a German victory. In hindsight, it is easy for most Americans to be appalled at German citizens vilifying the American president and cheering for a German victory, even sending money to Germany and some volunteering to serve in its army—but that is hindsight. At the time, most of Cincinnati's non-German community felt that the war had little to do with them, and they were generally sympathetic to the city's German-American population with relatives and acquaintances plunged into war. Participation and support of German causes were both a means of showing solidarity to loved ones and the fatherland and an attempt at swaying public opinion. It was not unpatriotic. America was officially neutral. Writing in a journal before the war, an unidentified Cincinnati German-American recorded the belief that as long as "speaking in German is practiced in this country, there exists no danger for peace with Germany…the day shall never come when we are compelled to raise our hand against the Motherland for the honor and defense of our new homeland." Beer garden bands showed support for Germany by alternately playing "Die Wacht am Rhein" and "The Star-Spangled Banner."

In 2010, World War I started ninety-six years ago. For perspective, this is only four fewer years than the number separating the cessation of the War of 1812 and the beginning of World War I. England as ally and Germany as foe is a mentality produced by the twentieth century. America's entry into the war on the Allied side would not have appeared inevitable from a bar stool in Over-the-Rhine in 1914. The *Freie Presse* argued on July 30, 1915, that if England won, the nation would "not rest until she destroyed the last possible competitor for the rule of the seas and the world markets." "There is sufficient room for both the United States and Germany on the seas, but the sea has not enough room for an unvanquished England and any other power. Germany's victory will save us a war."

Nor was criticism of Wilson unjustified. When the *Volksblatt* wrote in the fall of 1915 that "if Wilson would be as conscientious in protecting German soldiers from United States bullets as English ships from German torpedoes, we would be celebrating victory," it had a point. Wilson's foreign policy was lopsided neutrality. It forbade Germany from using submarine warfare, their strongest tactical defense against the English navy, at the same time that it was permitting large amounts of munitions to be manufactured in the United States and shipped to England—on ships protected from attack by the prohibition on submarine warfare. The munitions production was also turning small East Coast towns into industrial boomtowns and giving the United States a financial stake in the war. During this period of "neutrality," members of Wilson's cabinet repeatedly made pro-British sentiments clear, and Wilson himself started to question the patriotism of the "hyphenates" (i.e., the German-Americans). Wilson stated, "I neither seek the favor nor fear the displeasure of that small alien element which puts loyalty to any foreign power before loyalty to the United States." While the nation was still "neutral," Wilson was suggesting that expressing support for Germany over England was anti-American.

In May 1915, the Germans sank an ocean liner full of both civilian passengers and English munitions. American citizens were among those killed on the *Lusitania*, and it represented a significant shift in Americans' attitudes about both the nation of Germany and the German-Americans within the United States. By August 1915, the *Volksblatt* wrote: "That opinion in American circles against the Germans has become such that it causes uneasiness…It is certainly not agreeable to live in an environment where one meets at every step hostile glances and perceived hidden animosity." However, little changed in the behavior or tone of Cincinnati's German-Americans. Over-the-Rhine saloons remained full of German pride.

On January 31, 1917, America learned that Germany was announcing submarine warfare with England, a move that would inevitably lead to America entering the war. Backpedaling and desperate machinations in the German-language press began. Earlier in January, the *Volksblatt* had confidently stated that Germany would not be foolish enough to evoke the ire of the United States by using subs. The day after the news that they would, the paper concluded that the move was clearly necessary in Germany's "fight for existence." By March, the paper was obviously reflecting a growing sense of fear in the German-American community of their fellow Cincinnatians: "We are convinced that our government will have no cause to complain about us; it is not to be expected that we will experience the least harassment." The paper was wrong.

In Apirl 1917, the *Volksblatt* stopped attacking Wilson and tried to provide more nuance to its position: "To support the United States is a duty. To support the President as representative of the United States is no less a duty; but to have to support England, that hypocritical robber nation, that hereditary enemy of our country, that's what makes us heartsick." The change in rhetoric was not enough. Police raided the paper's office in October. Afterward, *Volksblatt* started repeatedly encouraging readers to buy war bonds.

In 1917, a majority of school board members still supported keeping German instruction in the schools, but the term of one of these favorable members was expiring. German societies put full support behind a candidate also known to support retention of German instruction. He won but refrained from showing up at the meeting when the vote was taken. Personal intimidation was assumed. Two other members switched their positions, and only one of the seven board members kept his conviction. German instruction was removed from the schools in February 1918. A considerable number of German instructors were terminated.

On April 3, 1918, the board of trustees of the library ordered the librarian to "make at once an exhaustive investigation of the books and periodicals… and remove…from circulation any and all books and periodicals in the leastwise containing any suggestions which might be considered or construed as favoring or supporting a pro-German propaganda." This was accomplished, and then the library went further. On May 8, the board ordered the removal of "all German books, periodicals and newspapers."

On April 9, 1918, over the objection of a solitary councilmember who characterized the action as "childish," Cincinnati City Council voted to change the names of thirteen streets. Among them, Over-the-Rhine's Bremen Street became Republic and Hamburgh became Stonewall. Also in April, the trend of changing business names reached its peak. Over-the-Rhine's German Mutual Insurance Company covered its German inscription and changed its name to the Hamilton County Insurance Company. The German National Bank on Vine Street became the Lincoln National Bank. These were just two of many.

Right: The German Mutual Insurance Company as it appears today. *From the collection of the Public Library of Cincinnati and Hamilton County.*

Below: The inscription "Deutshe Gegens Versicherungs Gesellschaft Von Cincinnati" was covered on the German Mutual Insurance Building of Cincinnati when the name was changed to the Hamilton County Insurance Company during the 1918 anti-German hysteria.

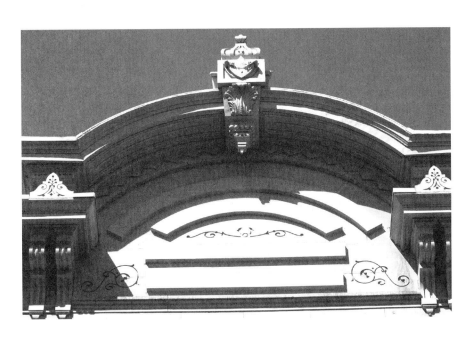

In June, all speeches and songs at a German society celebration had to be delivered or sung in English by order of the chief of police. Cincinnati police detectives were present at the event to assure that the orders were followed.

A.B. Heilman, president of the Findlay Market Improvement Association, arranged to have bands play concerts of patriotic music at the market. He explained that "we are going to show we are real Americans."

A problem with livestock in Kansas also had an impact on Over-the-Rhine's fate—at least it was *probably* Kansas. An influenza virus, believed to have been a combination of a swine and fowl virus, broke out among World War I troops in 1918. It was given the name the "Spanish flu" because the first honest reports of it came from Spanish troops, but it is actually believed to have originated in Kansas and been spread throughout Europe by American troops. Regardless of its origins, it was an unprecedented pandemic. It killed 675,000 people in the United States alone (when the country had about one-third of its current population). The "great influenza" killed more people in a year than the Black Plague killed in a century, and it did so roughly corresponding with the anti-German hysteria. This compounded both the atmosphere of fear as well as a face-saving reason for Cincinnati's German-Americans to cancel or refuse to attend German society events. Some stopped attending society events with the admission that they feared repercussion. Others blamed the flu, and many events were cancelled by order of the Health Department.

It is easy to look back on the anti-German hysteria with an inadequate understanding of what it must have been like to live through it. Changing some street names does not sound particularly frightening in hindsight—just stupid. But it went much deeper. The unquestioning, Toby Keith, pop culture form of patriotism that is common today was essentially invented during World War I. Before that, it was far more common to believe that Americans could retain an independent ethnic identity consistent with American patriotism. The war brought a new type of nationalism and a wave of nativist hatred that was both familiar and unprecedented, and it shifted very quickly against the Germans. Prior to 1915, most nativist, anti-immigrant sentiment was aimed at the newer Eastern European immigrants, but when the war started almost all of that was forgotten. Theodore Roosevelt suggested hanging or shooting any German-American who showed disloyalty to America. Congress passed the vaguely worded Espionage Act in June 1918 that made it a criminal offense to say things to aid the enemy or obstruct the war effort; and the Justice Department gave semiofficial support to a private organization called the American Protective League to help enforce the act. League members all took an oath, received an official-looking badge and reported suspicious activity. Its "operatives" also initiated ad hoc "investigations" of people who failed to buy war bonds or expressed "seditious and disloyal utterances." This volunteer counter-espionage group failed to identify a single actual spy, but regardless of how laughable it may have been, it would have been intimidating to German-Americans. The ASL's army of volunteer sleuths claimed to grow to 250,000 throughout the United States. Its tentacles permeated almost every community and harassed and intimidated countless innocent citizens. Nationwide, German-Americans were attacked at random, beaten, their possessions destroyed. In at least one harrowing case in Illinois, a man was lynched by a mob solely for his ethnicity, and a jury acquitted the flag-adorned murderers.

Due largely to the number and social stature of German-Americans in Cincinnati, there were no acts of overt violence, but that does not mean that the threat was anything other than deadly serious. In his 1965 doctoral thesis about the social disintegration of Over-the-Rhine's German community, Guido Andre Dobbert concludes:

> *To a certain extent the Germans' situation in Cincinnati was similar to the Jews in Germany during the very early stages of Nazi persecution. It was not so much the acts of physical violence, though in Germany there were enough of those, but the dread thereof and the knowledge that the public at large would idly stand by, either approving or indifferent, in the presence of misdeeds perpetrated by a small group of deranged fanatics.*

Before the war, summer in Over-the-Rhine was filled with parades on Sundays to and from festivals and picnics, and winters were full of balls, concerts and "entertainment of every kind imaginable." That all ended with the American entry into the war. Change that had already occurred made the destruction of the neighborhood's German culture easier. It had already become more ethnically diverse. Socioeconomic status defined its residents more than ethnicity, and the German-American upper class had abandoned it for the hilltops. Two things kept it German and kept it vibrant: the presence of Cincinnati's German societies and its hundreds of saloons serving a seemingly endless supply of great local beer. The Great War effectively ended both.

THE ROAD TO DRYVILLE

"Temperance" and "prohibition" refer to different periods with different focuses. In fact, what "temperance" meant changed during different periods of history, and "prohibition" exchanged its lowercase "p" for an uppercase "P" when it turned from a battle fought on the state level to a push for a Prohibition Amendment to the U.S. Constitution. These were national movements with local branches. Clearly, their scope far exceeds an early history of Over-the-Rhine, but it is difficult to imagine a neighborhood more impacted by Prohibition than Over-the-Rhine. The neighborhood was the center of Cincinnati Germandom, and Cincinnati's German-Americans had become increasingly focused on the political issues surrounding drink. Beer was the glue that continued to make Over-the-Rhine the social center of the city's German-American community. The neighborhood's hundreds of saloons and the roughly dozen breweries in or near it still rolled out the Gemütlichkeit nightly. Beer was the center of the neighborhood's culture and its economy. By the early part of the twentieth century, Over-the-Rhine had undergone significant social changes. It had become solidly working class and a lot more ethnically diverse, but it retained its identity and its vibrancy through the German societies and its ample German lager. When both were destroyed, Over-the-Rhine ceased to be Over-the-Rhine.

Prohibition didn't come from nowhere. The Eighteenth Amendment and the Volstead Act were the pinnacle of victory for antialcohol forces that had been at work since the early nineteenth century. The first temperance society was formed in 1813. In the very early years, the movement was dominated by the rich. Back then, "temperance" usually meant moderation. Social, moderate consumption of beer and wine was fine, even encouraged. The movement had a classist undertone. The problem wasn't alcohol. The problem was a lower-class abuse of alcohol. Both the class makeup and the message changed with time. By the 1830s, the movement was composed more of the middle class. It was a self-help movement, and it started to increasingly push total abstinence. Unlike later prohibition campaigns, earlier nineteenth-century temperance movements did not try to make alcohol illegal; they tried to persuade people to stop drinking for religious and moral reasons. The tactic was called "moral suasion," and it focused largely on what alcohol did to families: took money from the household, led to domestic abuse and deprived children of a loving, responsible father. Some

Early temperance propaganda focused on moral suasion, frequently depicting the toll drink took on children and families. Its goal was the choice of abstinence. As temperance turned into prohibition movements, the focus turned to saloons. *From the collection of the Public Library of Cincinnati and Hamilton County.*

temperance advocates still maintained a belief that moderate drinking was acceptable, and even people who advocated complete abstinence thought that laws that tried to force abstinence on others were unrealistic.

As middle-class temperance leaders started telling the rich that their wine had to go along with the laborers' whiskey, the movement started losing the support of the upper class. Temperance advocates also started developing a relatively constant profile along ethnic and geographic lines. Temperance people were Anglo, Protestant and tended to have been born in the United States, and the movements had their strongest support in small towns or rural areas. They were also churchgoers, and religion came to play a large role in the antialcohol crusades.

The strategy of temperance advocates shifted in the 1850s from moral suasion to political and legal action. Over 1.5 million immigrants arrived in America during the 1840s, and roughly 78 percent of them were Irish or German. Cincinnati's population increased from 46,000 in 1840 to 115,000 in 1850, and the city went from being overwhelmingly native born to having a 44 percent immigrant population. The Germans and the Irish didn't share the same attitude that the native-born Anglo population had about alcohol. They liked to drink. It was part of their culture, of the enjoyment of life, and they attached no moral failing to the enjoyment of drink. In fact, the German churches often had rathskellers so that parents could drink together after church while their children were in Sunday school classes.[6] This made moral suasion particularly ineffective on this population of new Americans.

At the same time the population of America was increasing and becoming more ethnically diverse, it was also becoming more urban. The 1840s saw the largest shift to urban life in the nation's history. In the Midwest, the proportion of people living in cities more than doubled from 3.9 percent to 9.2 percent. New, rapidly growing urban centers gave birth to a new institution—the saloon. Saloons became the center of social life for working-class urbanites, particularly immigrants. They also became the central target for temperance advocates.

For temperance advocates, saloons represented the epitome of the evil of alcohol. Early immigrants were frequently single men, and the saloon provided a male-dominated social structure. The right saloons could even

---

6. Old St. Mary's, the city's oldest church, located at Twelfth and Clay, still maintains its rathskeller and still conducts a Mass in German.

Saloons were the dominion of men, places for card games, cigars, conversation and drink. *Courtesy of the Cincinnati Historical Society Library, Cincinnati Museum Center.*

provide female companionship at a reasonable hourly rate. Even when patrons were married, the saloon could be the focal point of a man's social life, and they could also capture a significant part of his paycheck. There were genuine links between drunkenness and domestic violence. And some saloons attracted criminals and gamblers. Crime rose as the nation became more urbanized. The immigrants who arrived in cities almost penniless and requiring social welfare were the same ethnic groups filling the saloons. The temperance movement linked all of these things together in a causal formula: alcohol led to the destruction of the family, the erosion of American (Anglo, Protestant) moral values, destitution, poverty and crime. If alcohol could be eliminated, almost all of society's social ills would disappear. Although this causal link between drink and the destruction of western civilization was simplistic, the saloon gave it a face; and that face was particularly ominous to the women who were barred from its dominion.

The saloon became a convenient, visible rallying cry. It also permitted a very effective shift in propaganda. Early temperance movements were based on self-improvement. Even later years placed responsibility on the drinker: moral suasion was about making drinkers rethink their life choices and become more responsible. Blaming the saloon owner made the drunk a victim. It also provided a location for protests that created powerful visual images. Although antialcohol movements existed from the early nineteenth century through Prohibition, the Woman's Crusade and the Woman's Christian Temperance Union (WCTU), founded in Hillsboro, Ohio, in 1873, launched such effective propaganda campaigns that it remains the visual image that most people associate with temperance.

Early legal approaches to prohibition were focused on the municipal and state levels and typically focused on licensing. The original Ohio constitution permitted licensing of liquor establishments, and the licensing practice was continued in significant 1831 modifications to the state constitution and legislation. This system typically gave licenses "to keepers of taverns or public inns" only after "twelve respectable landholders" testified "that the applicant was worthy, of good reputation, had suitable accommodations, and that a public inn or tavern was necessary at the place proposed." The City of Cincinnati's original municipal ordinance also contained licensing provisions. Most of the requirements mirrored state law, but Cincinnati defined a tavern by setting a minimum standard for accommodation of travelers. It also specifically permitted the licensing of "coffee houses" or "porter houses" (what would later be called saloons) that lacked the accommodations of taverns, but like taverns, these establishments needed to present a petition to city council with the oath of twelve citizens stating that the proposed owner was "an orderly and suitable person" and an explanation of why this establishment at its proposed location would benefit the community. Annual city license fees ranged from twenty-five to seventy-five dollars in 1828.

Licensing generated revenue for the state and regulated the number and types of establishments selling liquor. Pressured by communities that wanted to push for complete criminalization of alcohol sales by denying licenses, the state constitution was amended in 1847 to let the license system be governed locally. With the new local option, Cincinnati tried municipal-level prohibition in 1847, but the experiment was short-lived. There were over 400 "coffee houses" in the city of Cincinnati in 1847, and the police force consisted of one city marshal and two deputies. They quickly gave up efforts to enforce the law. Other communities must have had similar experiences, because the local license system was repealed in 1848 and replaced with no governing law at all. Cincinnati returned to licensing and generated $23,704 in city revenue from 504 saloons in 1849; but on a state level, dry forces succeeded in amending the Ohio constitution to prohibit the state from establishing a licensing system. A court in the 1880s noted that the lack of a licensing system was the result of the "extremists" on both sides of the liquor question with a result that "disappointed both." However, it seems to have disappointed the drys more than the wets because it essentially led to the unregulated proliferation of saloons. It also caused Over-the-Rhine and other immigrant wards to get organized and make sure that they established and maintained liquor-friendly city councils.

The 1840s also saw the beginning of statewide prohibition attempts. These either focused on licensing or outright prohibition. The first state law was passed in Maine in 1851, forever branding state constitutional approaches to prohibition as "Maine laws." When Ohio formed a constitutional delegation to reexamine the state constitution in 1851, Cincinnati's Germans and Irish played a critical role in quashing a prohibition-friendly slate of delegates. Urban German and Irish wards, including those in and around Over-the-Rhine, continued to provide the votes needed to block state prohibition attempts in successive years. Thanks largely to its immigrant population, Ohio never followed Maine's lead, but several other states did. These early experiments in prohibition were both unpopular and unsuccessful. The laws were enforced ineffectively, and some observers said that crime actually rose in dry states. A revolt led by the Irish in Maine caused it to repeal its own "Maine law," and state prohibition had been repealed in every state that attempted it by the start of the Civil War.

Following the Civil War, prohibition seemed like an idea whose time had come and gone. Many rural soldiers became exposed to drinking and male saloon culture for the first time during the war, and large numbers of them decided that they liked it. German-Americans were also noted for valor and patriotism during the war. This helped remove some of the nativist stigma on German-American culture and made non-Germans more comfortable with entering German neighborhoods like Over-the-Rhine and enjoying the increasingly popular German lager beer. Both state and municipalities were also starting to understand that they couldn't afford to outlaw alcohol even if they wanted to.

By the time of the Woman's Crusade in 1873, the distilling and brewing industries had a capital investment in the city of over $33,000,000, and the number of saloons exceeded two thousand. Directly and indirectly, the alcoholic beverage industry was estimated to employ between thirty and forty thousand Cincinnatians. In 1875, one-third of the nation's federal tax revenue came from beer and whiskey, and by the 1890s, Cincinnati was paying more of this tax than any other district in America. Distilleries in Cincinnati, Covington and Newport paid one-sixth of the entire internal revenue of the United States in 1897. Brewing accounted for less total tax revenue, but it was one of the largest industries in Cincinnati, producing 1,325,000 barrels of beer annually by the later part of the 1890s. Locally, the tax on beer alone amounted to $1,250,000 in tax revenue.

The positive economic impact that alcohol had on society did not sway prohibitionists. They believed that the elimination of the social ills attributable to alcohol would easily offset some lost tax revenue, and most had little sympathy for people who chose to earn a living making, dealing or pushing liquid evil. Denied outright prohibition, dry Ohio legislators started passing legislation to whittle away at personal liberty. The Ohio Constitution of 1851 had been drafted to state: "No license to traffic intoxicating liquors shall hereafter be granted in this state, but the general assembly may, by law, provide against evils resulting therefrom." At their least creative, new pieces of legislation dramatically increased fines and penalties for selling on Sundays or breaking the common labor law. They also tried to better regulate behavior inside saloons. It became a crime to buy a drink for "a person who is at the time intoxicated, or in the habit of getting intoxicated." Furnishing alcohol to a minor became illegal. Anyone who recalls the "just say no" campaigns of the 1980s ("this is your brain on pot") can imagine the nature of class materials used to fulfill a state statute that required instruction on "the nature of alcoholic drinks and narcotics, and their effects on the human system in connection with the subjects of physiology and hygiene." Textbooks were approved by politically powerful temperance groups, and the law required firing school staff who refused to teach the material.

The Schaefer Law tried to cut down on saloon business by criminalizing the practice of giving away free food at saloons, "except crackers, cheese and pretzels," but the law was struck down when Foucar's on Walnut challenged its constitutionality. The court ruled that a law that prevented Foucar's from giving away roast beef was "unwarrantable and unjust discrimination and certainly opposed to the American spirit of fair play and a square deal." Roast beef went back up on the Foucar's bar.

Laws regulating sexual behavior also provided power in saloon settings. Using foul language in front of a female was the same criminal offense as exposing yourself to her. (Both were punishable by a fine of up to twenty dollars and twenty days in jail.) Prostitution was illegal, but trying to go the other route could get an amorous man in even more trouble—and so could being the bartender of the wrong couple. Section 7023a of the Ohio Revised Code said:

> *Whoever in a wine-room, saloon or restaurant, or elsewhere furnishes to any female of good repute for chastity, over eighteen years of age, or to any female under eighteen years of age, any wine or other intoxicating liquors, with intent thereby to enable himself to have sexual intercourse, or to aid or assist any person in accomplishing or having sexual intercourse with such female, shall be imprisoned in the penitentiary not more than three years nor less than one year.*

The most devastating laws enacted to combat the evils resulting from intoxicating liquors were the local option laws. In 1888, legislation was passed to permit both municipalities and townships outside of municipalities to vote themselves dry. If one-quarter of voters in a township signed a petition calling for a vote, a special election was held. If a simple majority voted the area dry, all alcohol sales had to stop within thirty days. There were no grandfather clauses. Your business simply became worthless. The law made going dry more palatable to rural folks by exempting "the manufacture and sale of cider, or sale of wine manufactured from the pure juice of the grape, cultivated in this state." Rural Ohioans made money on vineyards and orchards, and they primarily drank hard cider. The exception let them vote against the German brewers, the predominately Jewish distillers and the saloon owners without putting a crimp in their own wholesome drinking choices.

As the local option law was written in 1888, it threatened business for local breweries, but they shrugged off the towns and rural townships that were never particularly lucrative territory to begin with. However, the law went much further after the turn of the century. In 1902, the Beal Law put more teeth in the local option, letting municipalities vote themselves dry. If the measure won, the city could not go wet for a minimum of two years, but if the measure lost, another petition could lead to another vote as soon as someone got enough signatures on another petition.

As problematic as the Beal Law was, it seemed tame in comparison to the 1904 Brannock Local Option Law. The previous local option laws were defined and limited by recognized political boundaries: towns, cities or townships. The Brannock Law permitted something far more devious: 40

percent of registered voters in a "residence district" could file a petition and cause a special election to be held within twenty to thirty days after the filing. The election would determine whether the "residence district" would vote itself dry. The key to the legislation was that the people filing the petition got to define their own "residence district." It had to be contiguous and had to contain between two hundred and two thousand people, but it could otherwise be gerrymandered in any way that would increase its chances of passage. The "residence district" could not include a block where more than half of the street footage was commercial, but saloons were not to be counted. As if all of this weren't enough, the law also said that parks and churches were to be counted as residential property. Like the Beal Law, a dry vote under the Brannock Law made this self-defined "residence district" dry for a minimum of two years, and all sales had to stop within thirty days; but failure to get a dry vote permitted another election if another petition was filed. In addition, only people who lived in the "residence district" could vote. Business owners could not. By the summer of 1905, some five hundred Ohio towns and cities had voted themselves dry, in whole or in part, through one of the local options. Hamilton County and Cincinnati stayed wet, but by the end of 1908, Preble, Warren and Clermont Counties had all gone completely dry.

Regardless of how inequitable or how much gerrymandering could be done, the legislation had no direct impact on Over-the-Rhine or the sopping wet city of Cincinnati in general, but it did start to dry up some local export markets for local breweries. There are two probable, indirect consequences of the advent of the local options. The vast majority of beer brewed in Cincinnati was consumed locally. This had been a luxury. Large brewers like Adolphus Busch in St. Louis had to be more dependent on exports because the area lacked the same density—and thirst—that Cincinnati had. This also made Busch a pioneer of beer exporting, being the first to use refrigerated rail cars and finding other ways to make the system more efficient and productive. Cincinnati breweries were less capable of using rail. When Busch built his brewery, he did so at a later time and in a less populated area than Over-the-Rhine. Most Cincinnati breweries were built on the canal and were surrounded by the most densely populated parts of the city. They were built on the canal to utilize river traffic. That made sense when they were constructed, but by the turn of the century it locked them into a dying mode of transportation. If they wanted to make up for beer sales lost to local options in Ohio, they needed to further saturate the city. The presence of so many saloons fueled temperance fires and led to a restriction on the number of liquor establishments by population.

In 1913, the Ohio legislature restricted the number of saloons that could exist within a city. No town or township of fewer than 500 people could have more than one saloon. At the turn of the century, the total number of saloons in Cincinnati still approached 2,000 and constituted one saloon for between every 160 to 170 residents.[7] Although Hamilton County's state senators and state representatives all voted against it, the law passed in April 1913, requiring the destruction of hundreds of businesses. By the time war broke out in Europe in 1914, the city was down to 778 saloons—still a lot, but down considerably from highs that exceeded 2,000.

A federal congressional resolution calling for a national Prohibition amendment to the U.S. Constitution had been introduced in Congress every year since 1876, but none even emerged from committee until the Hobson Amendment reached the floor of the House of Representatives in 1914. The resolution failed to get the necessary two-thirds vote needed for a constitutional amendment, but it did win a narrow majority of votes in the House. Legally it was defeated, but it was a huge moral victory for the Prohibitionists. Once considered a pipe dream of fanatics, nationwide Prohibition was nearing reality. During the war, a number of factors pushed it over the edge.

Temporary taxes had been imposed on alcohol to help pay for the Revolutionary War and the War of 1812, but both measures were allowed to sunset. When President Lincoln brought back the alcohol tax in 1862 to pay for the Civil War, it never went away. The United States Brewers League (later the United States Brewers Association) was formed to address issues with the tax, including a provision that would have levied the tax on beer already produced and already under contracts negotiated under pretax costs. The brewers did not, however, oppose the tax generally. In fact, they began to see how important it was to their self-preservation and later revised history to claim that the organization was formed for purely patriotic reasons to help the government implement the tax. For most of the three decades following the Civil War, the annual federal tax on alcohol provided at least

---

7. In 1890, there were 1,810 saloons and the city's population was 297,000, one saloon for every 164 inhabitants, or roughly every 41 adult males.

20 percent of federal tax revenues, and much more in some years. When the tax was doubled during the Spanish-American War, the brewers said that they had paid for 40 percent of the costs of the war. By the fall of 1910, the federal government was receiving $80 million a year from taxes on beer sales alone. Nationally, there were over 1,500 breweries employing roughly fifty thousand people.

In 1895, the U.S. Supreme Court declared the income tax unconstitutional. That made tax on alcohol absolutely indispensible to maintaining the federal government and ensured that Prohibition would never happen. That changed when the states ratified the Sixteenth Amendment in 1913, paving the way for the income tax and permitting America to survive without alcohol revenue.

Woman's suffrage was another key component in making Prohibition a reality. The Woman's Christian Temperance Crusade occurred in 1873–74. It didn't last long, and it did little to change the attitudes of Cincinnatians. When the crusaders attempted to organize a march in front of the Foss, Schneider & Brenner brewery, they got pelted with eggs and doused with beer from men hanging out of brewery windows. They drew so much vitriol in the streets that the police officer assigned to guard them had to draw his pistol three times to keep angry crowds at bay, and the mayor forbade them from marching again. When they ignored the mayor's orders and tried to march the following day, they were all arrested, quickly ending their attempts to change hearts and minds in the "Paris of America." They were, however, far more effective in other places and on a national level. In 1874, the United States Brewers Association blamed the Crusade for the first-ever annual decline in beer production, stating: "Very severe is the injury which the brewers have sustained in the so-called temperance states." The Crusade was not the beginning of female involvement in the temperance movement. Women had been involved in supportive roles from the beginning and even engaged in a series of violent attacks on saloon property in the 1850s. The Crusade was just a very successful propaganda campaign, and it also marked a shift in strategy. The WCTU became a powerful political force and started linking women's right to vote with prohibition. The two things didn't necessarily go hand in hand, but both the WCTU and the brewers engaged in a course of action and exchange of rhetoric that helped cement the connection.

"VOTE WET FOR MY SAKE!"

"VOTE DRY FOR MINE!"

Which shall it be, which shall it be.
The Big Fat Brewer, or the Poor Family?
Vote YES on PROHIBITION Nov. 5.

Union Club.
Chas. Mayer, Pres.

A. Y. Rehl.
Chair. Pub. Com.
—Advertisement.

Particularly after the commencement of World War I, the successful tactic of targeting saloons as the enemies of women, children and stable families was extended to the brewers. The caption reads: "Which shall it be, which shall it be. The Big Fat Brewer, or the Poor Family? Vote YES on PROHIBITION Nov. 5."

Members of the women's temperance movement had a particular hatred for Germans and beer. Even the Irish were largely ignored. The enemy was the German saloonkeeper and brewer. This may have begun with xenophobia, but it was exacerbated by the brewers themselves. They frequently took strong, vocal and insulting positions on women's suffrage, making enemies of women who might have been opposed to Prohibition, or at least neutral to it, if the brewers didn't help crystallize the link between suffrage and Prohibition through their own propaganda, frequently condemning "fanatical" Prohibitionists and suffragists in the same sentence. When the right to vote was attained, women overwhelmingly used the power against the sexist German brewers. States that gave women the right to vote started seeing themselves go dry—seven of them during a three-year stretch in the 1910s.[8]

Suffrage was not the only area where the strategic and public relations choices made by the brewers backfired. Given all of the other forces that were at work, Prohibition might have been inevitable, but the brewers would have put up a much better fight if they had been better at building a coalition with distillers and saloon owners. Instead, they tossed whiskey and hard

---

8. The Nineteenth Amendment gave women the right to vote. It was not ratified as part of the U.S. Constitution until 1920, but states started adopting women's suffrage prior to the constitutional requirement that they do so.

liquor under the bus. They tried to promote beer as an alternative to liquor, even promoting it as healthy. Beer, they claimed, was not only a healthful alternative, it was even good for the sick and pregnant women. It helped digestion. Hard liquor, by contrast, was linked by the brewers to crime and vice. When the Wilson administration limited the alcohol content of beer to 2.75 percent as a war measure in 1918, brewers sucked up the blow, put on a proud face and welcomed the opportunity to be the low-alcohol alternative to injurious intoxicants. The problem with this strategy was twofold. First, it didn't work. In the 1875 *History of the Great Temperance Movement*, Reverend Shaw proselytized: "Perhaps you are in sympathy with these brewers and say, that if people would take beer instead of alcohol, drunkenness would cease. But for the vast majority who drink, beer is only introductory to something stronger. It is only one carriage in the same funeral. Do not spell it B-e-e-r but spell it B-i-e-r. May the lightnings of Heaven strike and consume all the breweries." There was no notable moderation wing of the temperance movement after roughly the 1840s.

Secondly, it played industries with identical interests against each other in a way that hurt both. The saloon was the real hobgoblin, and by 1909, 70 percent of American saloons were either owned by, in debt to or otherwise linked to a brewery. In Cincinnati, calculating how many saloons were controlled by brewers as Prohibition neared seems impossible because state law prevented a person or entity, or members of a corporate board, from holding an interest in more than one saloon. The statute was broadly written, forbidding any applicant for a saloon license from being "in any way interested in the business conducted at any other place where intoxicating liquors are sold or kept for sale." By legal necessity, arrangements would have been informal, but saloons were "loyal" to one brewer, and saloon owners were often called the pawns of brewers, so regardless of the nature of the agreements, public perception linked the brewers with the saloons; and Prohibitionists held brewers accountable for

In 1889, the John Hauck Brewery was pushing the image of its beer as a temperate alternative to hard liquor. *From the collection of the Public Library of Cincinnati and Hamilton County.*

All Ye Invalids !
All Ye Weak ! !
All Ye Dyspeptics !!!

Improve and complete your
health by partaking of our
excellent

Invalid Bottle Beer.

The JOHN HAUCK BREWING CO.

CINCINNATI, O.

The following year, Hauck was pushing the
"medicinal" effects of its beer. *From the collection of
the Public Library of Cincinnati and Hamilton County.*

the activities that occurred within the saloons. Hard liquor interests took advantage of this. While brewers linked crime to hard liquor, liquor interests linked it to the saloon culture and suggested that reduction in their total number and better control of these facilities was the answer to preventing crime.

This infighting within the alcoholic beverage industry was in stark contrast to the tactics of the Anti-Saloon League (ASL). The ASL had become adroit at a strategy called the "Ohio Idea" that combined disparate forces under one, limited agenda. By limiting its agenda and focus, and not getting too picky about its bedfellows, the ASL had combined the strengths of the suffragists, the nativists, the progressives and the Ku Klux Klan (who feared whiskey in the hands of blacks). Together, they put all other differences aside and joined forces to accomplish a single, shared goal—Prohibition.

The United States Brewers Association was the most organized force opposing Prohibition, but it made critical errors in judgment and public relations. In hindsight, giving significant support to the German National Alliance was one of the largest mistakes. In the later part of the 1800s, an increasing number of local and state organizations was created to celebrate an annual German Day. Existing German-American societies, as well as new ones, were formed for other purposes but also played a role in the celebrations, and all of these groups organized local and regional federations. Formal hierarchies were established for the organizations; and in 1901, delegates from state groups met to form a national body that would oversee forty-seven state organizations that, in turn, oversaw numerous local societies. The German American Alliance was officially incorporated by an act of Congress in 1907. It existed to promote issues important to German-Americans. This included such benign roles as erecting statues and plaques to commemorate the accomplishments of German-Americans, supporting physical education in schools, forestry conservation and encouraging German immigrants to attain full citizenship. It also included lobbying on state and federal levels for issues including German language instruction in public schools, opposing immigration restrictions and opposing restrictions on personal liberty. Local alliance affiliates, like Cincinnati's Stadtverband, endorsed candidates, and both the national organization and its affiliates played critical roles in quashing state prohibition campaigns.

In addition to increasingly draconian local option laws, the early twentieth century saw more states going dry. Georgia voted itself dry in 1907, and it was quickly followed by five other states. Personal liberty came to the forefront of German National Alliance concerns. The relationship between the alliance and the United States Brewers Association became so close that many people viewed the alliance as nothing more than a puppet of the brewers. Undeniably, there was a close relationship. The Brewers Association paid for the alliance's Washington office, and the alliance was its most powerful lobbying force. When war broke out in Europe, the alliance was primarily focused on fighting Prohibition. It was a viable force, pulling power and money from an estimated three million members as Prohibition loomed. The German National Alliance was a good friend to have—until everything changed. By making personal liberty the universal rallying cry of Germandom in America, and by establishing the German National Alliance as the leading voice for the brewing industry, the brewers succeeded in making beer and German synonymous. Therefore, somewhere around the time that a torpedo slammed into the hull of the *Lusitania* in 1915, the pre-Prohibition brewers began their own sinking journey into oblivion.

Early temperance proponents preached self-control. Later temperance movements focused on the victimization of the drinker by the saloon owner, and this was supplemented by the demonization of "the liquor trade." During World War I, the tactically savvy Prohibition movement trained its sights squarely on the brewers—and went for the jugular. The platform of the German National Alliance included not only maintaining and safeguarding "the good relations existing between America and the old German fatherland," but it also included the limitation that nothing it does should be "inconsistent with the common good of the country" or not "in full accord with good citizenship." Nevertheless, congressional hearings began in February 1918 aimed at revoking the organization's charter. Conducted with full political theatre, the hearings ran through April. During the hearings, German-American witnesses were berated and insulted, and the press slanderously referred to members as "spies and suspects." Seeing an inevitable fate, the German American Alliance "voluntarily" disbanded in April 1918. The move was preemptive to Congress's official revocation of the alliance charter on July 2, 1918. As Prohibition votes neared, the brewers' most powerful public and political force was castrated and publicly branded as traitorous.

In the Civil War and the Spanish-American War, drinking beer was almost a patriotic act since alcohol taxes contributed so significantly to funding the wars. World War I became a very different story. A September 22, 1917 edition of the *Cincinnati Post* declared: "The liquor traffic in America is linked in action with the great German spy system for the destruction of American liberties." Editorials started popping up that referenced the "number of disloyal Americans [that] live Over-the-Rhine." Prohibition forces countered any arguments about alcohol taxes supporting the war effort with charges that the use of grain for brewing was starving troops. The claim was ridiculous. American grain harvests were plentiful, and breweries were only projected to use three-tenths of 1 percent of the national production in 1919. Nevertheless, the Wilson administration gave credibility to the claim by ordering breweries to cease all grain use on October 1, 1918.

The attacks on Cincinnati's beer barons must have been personally painful for the families. Many of them were noted for their civic responsibility, giving generously to the German old age home, the orphan asylum and other charitable causes. The John Hauck family saved the Cincinnati Zoo from bankruptcy. The Kauffman family donated the statue of St. Francis that adorns the front of St. Francis Cathedral on Liberty and Vine. The Moerlein family donated the pipe organ in Phillipus Church on McMicken, and the Moerlein family was noted for their charitable generosity. While other captains of industry were revered, these men and their families had become the targets of vicious attacks. Their commitment to their communities and their hard-earned success were used against them. Their ethnicity and their business were both cause for vilification.

The U.S. Constitution is not easy to change. After receiving a two-thirds vote from both houses of Congress, an amendment must also be ratified by three-fourths of the state legislatures. The Eighteenth Amendment began its journey through the states in 1918. Due, in part, to disproportionately drawn congressional districts, as well as all of the factors that made Prohibition politically expedient at that moment in time, more than 80 percent of the nation's legislators voted in favor of the amendment. On January 16, 1919, the United States Constitution was amended for the eighteenth time in history to include the following: "After one year from the ratification of this article the manufacture, sale, or transportation of intoxicating liquors within, the importation thereof into, or the exportation thereof from the United States and all territory subject to the jurisdiction thereof for beverage purposes is hereby prohibited."

The provision making the amendment take effect one year after ratification was a bone tossed to legislators who were concerned that the Constitution was being amended in a manner that made almost all breweries, distilleries, saloons and related businesses virtually worthless without any compensation to owners. The one-year period was a compromise to provide a time of transition. The phrase "intoxicating liquors" was also legislative art. It intentionally required interpretation. While Prohibition forces were obtaining ratification, some moderates held hope that the term would be defined strictly. It wasn't. While amending the Constitution was hard enough to require some compromise and ambiguity in the amendment, getting ordinary legislation like the Volstead Act passed only required a simple majority vote of Congress. The act carved out large exceptions to garner necessary support for passage, including the sacrificial wine exception and exempting hard cider, but it made the definition of "intoxicating" include any beverage with more than a 0.5 percent alcohol content. It also prohibited the use of the phrase "near beer," adding one more hurdle to marketing a product that nobody really saw as an alternative to real beer regardless of what you called it.

Ohio entered Prohibition before the January 16, 1920 federal deadline. Cincinnati went officially dry on May 27, 1919. Due to licensing, most establishments closed on Saturday, May 24. Only fourteen Cincinnati saloons paid the $305 license fee to stay open the three extra days. Most considered it cost-prohibitive, but the limited number that shelled out the fee cashed in, reporting sales on the final day ranging from $15,000 to $150,000. Kentucky stayed wet for another month. Those who could afford it stocked up liquor cabinets and wine cellars, but many just faced the necessity of sobriety—at least temporarily.

On March 29, 1919, the Bellevue Brewery was the first to close its doors as a direct result of Prohibition. The John Hauck Brewery sold property that was probably a saloon on Eastern Avenue, and the Kauffman brewery disposed of a similar property in Lockland. Then came the breweries themselves. Kauffman's Vine Street brewery was sold on August 28, 1920.

The Mohawk Brewery followed on March 29, 1921. Christian Moerlein, one of the largest breweries in America, tried to stay open producing near beer but succumbed to dry society. The company suspended operations on June 1, 1919, and portions of the brewery's massive complex were sold off in separate transactions during 1922.

An 1895 guide to Cincinnati lamented the passing of Over-the-Rhine's beer garden glory days following the Civil War, noting that it had lost most of its glamour. The guide prophesied: "In all probability the canal which marks its boundaries will also soon pass away and be converted into either a grand boulevard or the road-bed for steam railways. But as long as the canal remains the regions beyond to the base of the hills will always be known as 'Over the Rhine.'"

The guide was wrong about the name. The loss of the canal didn't change it, but it was right about the substance of the prediction. In 1920, the city

The subway being constructed in the drained canal bed next to the former Bellevue Brewery, originally located in a bend in the canal. Unused subway tunnels still sit under this bend in Central Parkway. *Courtesy of the Archives and Rare Books Library, University of Cincinnati.*

The Bellevue Brewery as it appears today. Central Parkway at its base was the Miami and Erie Canal. At the turn of the century, this intersection at Mohawk-Brighton was one of the busiest in the city.

started draining the canal to build a subway covered by a grand boulevard called Central Parkway. By then, the neighborhood's name was almost all that was left. Its German societies had been scattered. Its breweries were shuttered. Its notorious nightlife had been silenced. Its characteristic German flavor had become tainted as traitorous during the war and considered offensive to returning soldiers afterward. It was the end. You could no longer go over the Rhine. It didn't exist anymore. It had been assimilated by force. "America" had won.

ROT AND REDEMPTION

Over-the-Rhine never recovered its position as the center of the city's German heritage. Physically, it almost froze in time. With very few exceptions, the vast majority of the neighborhood's buildings were erected between the first wave of German immigration in the 1830s and the start of World War I. Physically, it still remains the German-American neighborhood that it was when it held the political power to change the outcome of city elections and served as the city's beloved and notorious German entertainment district. Socially, it has become a very different place. Although construction essentially froze in time, the people did not. Waves of Appalachian immigrants in the mid-1900s dramatically changed Over-the-Rhine, and so did a shift in racial composition that occurred in the later part of the twentieth century. These stories are as compelling as the story of the neighborhood's original era, but they are the stories of human struggles in a place that had become obsolete; they are the stories of battles over the vision of what to do with the deteriorating remains of a vanquished culture.

Over-the-Rhine never truly regained its pre-Prohibition status as a brewing center, but there were valiant attempts to keep Cincinnati's brewing industry alive. Immediately after Prohibition arrived, several of the breweries tried to survive on near beer products and soft drinks. The market for near beer spiked immediately after the enactment of Prohibition and then rapidly declined and was essentially dead in a few years. Christian Moerlein's near beer Chrismo didn't sell. Crown Brewery's Tang was also a flop, and the brewery closed in 1925. Hudepohl gave up on its Dutch Cocktail in 1928

By the arrival of Prohibition, Over-the-Rhine was already a pretty dismal collection of cramped tenements. *Courtesy of the Archives and Rare Books Library, University of Cincinnati.*

and relegated itself to becoming the distributor of a more popular Louisville near beer. Bruckmann was the only local brewer still making a near beer at the end of Prohibition. Some of the breweries, undoubtedly like hundreds of the saloons, approached Prohibition in essentially the same manner that they had approached Sunday closing laws: they elected not to be bound by it. Schaller's Main Street Brewery continued to make "near beer" of higher-than-legal alcohol content, and the Mohawk Brewery was raided by liquor agents in 1925 for making full-strength beer.

Many in the city's saloon businesses also tried to cling to life. Writing in the mid-1920s, Frank Grayson cryptically described the "passing of Wielert's" as being of a "comparatively recent date." Grayson informs: "The old place never suffered the ignominy of a police raid until after the prohibition barrier to personal liberty was raised. Then the place drooped, languished and gently breathed its last." Grayson uses similarly vague but instructive descriptions and phrases to indicate that various Over-the-Rhine establishments were still open past the enactment of Prohibition. Of the city's 800 saloons still in business

The Crown
Brewery attempted
to survive
Prohibition making
a near beer named
"Tang," but the
popularity of near
beer waned quickly
after Prohibition
began. *Courtesy of
Steven Hampton,
president, Brewery
District CURC.*

when Prohibition went into effect, 560 remained open after the Volstead Act became law. Some sold ice cream or sodas. Some undeniably continued to be saloons operated largely as before, but the Volstead Act was federal law, and the Eighteenth Amendment gave concurrent enforcement powers to both state and federal officials. A city as wet as Cincinnati didn't go truly dry overnight, but staying open during Prohibition was trickier than keeping a side door open on Sunday in violation of a law that nobody had ever taken seriously.

As passage of the Eighteenth Amendment loomed, the brewing and distilling industries represented nearly $1 billion in invested capital, making alcoholic beverages the nation's fifth-largest industry. Estimating the economic impact of Prohibition on the nation, Cincinnati or even just Over-the-Rhine seems impossible. First, it didn't happen in a vacuum. The men slaughtered on the World War I battlefields and many of those who died from the Spanish flu undoubtedly offset unemployment numbers in brewery, distilling and related jobs that many of them would have otherwise held. Secondly, it didn't happen overnight. Even before the Eighteenth Amendment was ratified, the Wilson administration was using the war as an excuse to cripple the brewing industry. In 1917, Wilson's fuel director announced that brewing production would have to be reduced by 30 percent to preserve grain stock and to alleviate overcrowded rail lines. Brewers agreed to reduce coal consumption to 50 percent of previous use, but this was insufficient to prevent Wilson's fuel administrator from announcing on July 10, 1918, that the breweries would be prohibited from buying any additional coal after current supplies were gone. On October 1, 1918, Wilson prohibited breweries from purchasing any additional grain until after the war, effectively halting all brewing operations when existing coal and grain were gone. Still unsatisfied, the president approved a measure that provided for a total ban on beer production regardless of remaining supplies on December 1, 1918.

Even after the Eighteenth Amendment was ratified in January 1919, it took a year to take effect, providing time for some people to find gainful new employment and a number of others to start businesses or be employed by businesses that would fail, but would not do so until later years. And, of course, Prohibition gave rise to new, illegal, undocumented career paths. Despite lackluster enforcement, violations of the Volstead Act were common. Enforcement reached its peak locally when 490 people were arrested for bootlegging in 1929.

JOHN THREM,

MANUFACTURER OF

Malt Shovels
BUNGS AND
Wooden Faucets,

—19—

West Canal St.,

Bet. Main and Walnut,

CINCINNATI,O.

Manufacturer of Cedar and Locust Faucets, Long Ice Chest Faucets, High Bungs. Mallets, Bung Starters, Corking Machines for Bottling. Hitching Posts, Wooden Screws, Whistle Bungs, and all other kinds of Turning done to order.

John Schmelzer & Son,

MANUFACTURERS OF SCHMELZER'S PATENT

BEER COOLERS,

—AND—

Butchers', Grocers' and Family

REFRIGERATORS.

AGENTS FOR THE

Standard Hydraulic Beer Pump and Regulator.

47 and 49 W. Canal St., CINCINNATI, O.

OFFICE AND SALOON FIXTURES A SPECIALTY.

This page: John Threm, manufacturer of malt shovels and beer taps, and John Schmelzer & Son, manufacturers of refrigerated beer coolers, are just two of numerous Cincinnati businesses that relied upon the production and consumption of beer to drive their manufacturing concerns. *From the collection of the Public Library of Cincinnati and Hamilton County.*

157

The unique and prominent role of breweries in the mid-1880s is reflected by this iron manufacturer ad that offers estimates for iron "used in the Construction of Buildings and Breweries." *From the collection of the Public Library of Cincinnati and Hamilton County.*

Like any massive social upheaval, there were winners and losers. Sometimes they were even the same people. The F.L. Emmert Grain Company provides a good example of how complicated the effects of Prohibition were on the economy. A Sunday edition of the *Commercial Gazette* in 1878 assessed the new idea of using brewers' grain for livestock feed. The article quotes a chemist who expresses approval of using brewers' grain for livestock, noting that the "brewers have long been noted for the care with which they select their grain" and that the "handling of it in the brewery is all that could be asked." When the grain leaves the brewery after the brewing process, it is "good for man and good for child, with nothing whatever in it that would injure the weakest." The topic was of interest to the brewers because their expanding operations were producing a growing quantity of spent grain, a byproduct that was expensive to haul away for disposal. Brewers shared this concern with F.L. Emmert over beers drank in the saloon that he owned with his father-in-law on the corner of Clifton and Vine. Which brewers shared this concern with Emmert is unrecorded, but the saloon would have been a matter of feet from the Moerlein family home on Mulberry Street, and the Christian Moerlein Brewery became the largest supplier of spent brewers' grains to F.L. Emmert's new business: he converted the saloon into a business that received, dried and sold spent grain for livestock feed.

The company moved to Dunlap Street in Over-the-Rhine and kept expanding operations in roughly the same location where they continue processing brewers' grains today. Although F.L. Emmert made it through Prohibition, it was a roller coaster ride. In the years before Prohibition, the company was getting about twenty-four dollars per ton for dried brewers' grain. When the Volstead Act became law, they saw the end and closed up shop, but brewers making near beer let them reopen in January 1920. Initially, the company did much better than survive. Business actually improved. F.L. Emmert Co. was not the only company to understand the money to be made processing brewers' grains, nor were its customers the only to understand the quality and value of the product. The death of the breweries caused a shortage of this quality livestock feed that many farmers and agricultural wholesale businesses had come to rely on. Requests for product—some with an almost desperate tone—came from Tennessee, South Carolina, New York, Pennsylvania and Wisconsin. At the beginning of April 1920, prices had risen to sixty-two dollars per ton, then seventy dollars per ton by the end of the month. In May, the company informed a customer, "We look for rapidly increasing prices…[and]…we will not sell futures at present quotations." Rather than listing prices, the company repeatedly told potential customers to make an offer, becoming accustomed to getting comfortably above market value. But what went up quickly came back down quickly. By mid-December 1920, a Tennessee customer that previously seemed grateful for fifty-five-dollars-per-ton pricing balked at paying forty-five dollars per ton.

A few years later, an F.L. Emmert employee sent four dollars in dues payments for its four remaining employees to the Association Against the Prohibition Amendment (AAPA). The AAPA was an anti-Prohibition lobbying group that targeted its fundraising campaigns on multimillionaires and people who had earned their living in alcohol-related industries. The F.L. Emmert Co. definitely fell into the second category. The company sent its four-dollar payment accompanied by a personal letter that read:

We are extremely sorry at this time not being able to help you financially as we would like to do, but our business has been such the past year that it is impossible for us to do so, not so much that we were not busy enough, but prices for our commodity were terrible, infact, [sic] most of our product was sold below cost of manufacture and…even at a loss….Nevertheless our sympathies are still with you and we appreciate the good work you are doing

*and sincerely hope that the time is close at hand for a real showdown and a
change, which surely will come eventually.*

The company's inability to continue operating with grain from near beer
production was clearly affected by the fact that almost no one was producing
or drinking it by the mid-1920s, but a letter from a company representative
to Nicholas Longworth, U.S. congressman representing Over-the-Rhine,
reflects some of the more complicated subplots of Prohibition. F.L. Emmert
Co. informed the congressman that it was becoming "utterly impossible" for
the company to compete in the livestock feed business because its product
was "a by-product of the breweries and as they are very busy in Canada,
they must dispose of some and are dumping quite a lot of it in our country
at a price that is far below our production cost." Although most of Canada
had enacted a form of Prohibition prior to the United States, it had even
bigger loopholes in it than the Volstead Act. Even though local provinces
could outlaw alcohol sales and consumption within their borders, the federal
Canadian government permitted the manufacture of alcoholic beverages.
It also permitted their cross-province and international exportation. This,
coupled with the United States' limited ability to control the policies of a
foreign government, made Canada a critical supplier of illegal booze to
American bootleggers. Prohibition created a boom in Canada's alcoholic
beverage industry that had impacts ranging in visibility and repercussion
from mob wars in Detroit and Chicago to threatening the solvency of the
F.L. Emmert Co. in Over-the-Rhine. Representative Longworth, who,
according to his wife, "did not have the slightest intention of complying with
the Eighteenth Amendment and never pretended to," may have wanted
to solve F.L. Emmert's problems through the repeal of Prohibition, but at
the time, all he offered in his return correspondence to the company was a
bureaucratic explanation about the process for filing tariff complaints.

While it is impossible to calculate an exact financial impact of Prohibition
on the economy of Over-the-Rhine, it was clearly devastating. The breweries
fell. Those that limped by did so as former shells of themselves. Saloons
closed. In addition to the direct loss of jobs in the brewing and distilling
industries; the direct loss in saloons, restaurants, theatres, bowling alleys
and other places of amusement; the indirect loss of jobs in grain and hop
storage, cooperage and related industries; as well as the loss of significant
tax revenue, the impact on land values must have also been dramatic.

Courtesy of Steven Hampton, president, Brewery District CURC.

Hundreds of buildings in Over-the-Rhine had been built to house saloons. The neighborhood was already undergoing change, a shift in demographics. By the turn of the century, its small, cramped, antiquated tenement housing stock was unappealing to most people who could afford to move to the hills. The profitability of saloons and the money funneled into them by brewers must have become an increasingly important factor in building valuations as well as the viability of businesses increasingly reliant on tourists and revelers from other parts of town. The economic impact would have been similar in Over-the-Rhine to what would happen to New Orleans's French Quarter if it were ordered dry overnight.

The impact on the social network is equally clear. Prohibition destroyed the societies that had already been silenced by the war. It destroyed both their sources of revenue and their social function. A Pioneer Society member noted: "Moist-happy sessions, jovial festivities are the live nerve for every society, without which in the long run it cannot thrive." In a society during Prohibition, "the minutes are read, the secretary replying monotonously: absent! After a good half hour it is time to go home. Such is the course of business." The fact that many of the members of German societies already lived outside of Over-the-Rhine, and that the neighborhood was becoming increasingly defined by social class across ethnic lines rather than by ethnicity, made it easy to destroy its Germanness. Before World War I, Over-the-Rhine was still critical to winning elections in Cincinnati, and its breweries were powerful economic engines. It was a bit disreputable, but it was beloved. All of that changed very abruptly between roughly 1917 and 1920. The neighborhood entered the 1920s unarguably adrift and in decline.

The answer to the timeline question being debated by the group of people standing out in front of Mike and Doug Booteses' brewery building in November 2009 is this: a matter of days after his inauguration, President Franklin Roosevelt requested that the new Congress revisit the definition of "intoxicating" in the Volstead Act. The prohibition against manufacture of any beverage containing more than 0.5 percent alcohol was replaced with language that permitted the manufacture and sale of 3.2 percent beer, effective April 7, 1933, except in states that elected to continue its ban. On the afternoon of December 5, 1933, Utah provided the final vote needed to ratify the Twenty-first Amendment, the amendment that reversed the Eighteenth and removed Prohibition from the U.S. Constitution.

Louis Hudepohl (born Ludwig Hudepohl II) had a business model that would raise a few eyebrows in modern state regulatory agencies. He had a combination real estate office and liquor store on Main Street. The real estate thing must not have worked out, because his business was listed solely as a wholesale liquor store a few years later; but he definitely had a bright future in the alcoholic beverage industry. Along with his partner, George Kotte, Hudepohl sold the liquor store on Main and bought a fledgling brewery on Buckeye Street (now East Clifton) in 1885. Born in Cincinnati by German immigrant parents, Hudepohl would become the first American-born member of Cincinnati's great pre-Prohibition beer barons. Although Louis Hudepohl died in 1902, his family-run brewery also bridged another

KREBS LITHO.CO. CINCINNATI.

Louis Hudepohl

The son of German immigrants, Louis Hudepohl II was Cincinnati's first American-born beer baron. He sold packaged liquor and wine and temporarily ran a real estate office out of a storefront on Main Street. With partner George Kotte, he bought the Buckeye Brewery, changing the brewery's name to Hudepohl after Kotte's death. *From the collection of the Public Library of Cincinnati and Hamilton County.*

generational gap: the Hudepohl Brewing Company was only one of four Cincinnati breweries to survive Prohibition. As the last to still be brewing near beer, the Bruckmann Brewing Company was the only Cincinnati brewery poised to immediately return to production of real beer. Hudepohl,

Foss-Schnieder and Schaller also resumed operations within a few months, and under their pre-Prohibition names. Within a year, these breweries were followed by a series of others that breathed new life into pre-Prohibition breweries. Windish-Muhlhauser's Lion Brewery became the Burger Brewery. The Gambrinus Stock facility reopened as the Vienna Brewing Company. George Weber's Jackson Brewery reopened as the Jackson Brewery. The Mohawk Brewery became the Clyffside Brewery. In the West End, Red Top was born in part of the John Hauck brewing complex, and Schoenling Brewery opened just north of the Burger facility.

Some of these breweries had more staying power than others. Foss-Schnieder lasted less than four years. Vienna Brewing Company folded in 1940, followed by Schaller's Main Street Brewery in 1941 and the Jackson Brewery in 1942. Bruckmann survived until 1949. Clyffside was purchased by Red Top in 1945. Using the Clyffside facility to increase its production, Red Top rose to become one of the largest breweries in Ohio, but consolidation and changes in the industry forced Red Top to close in 1957, leaving only Hudepohl continuing commercial brewing operations in Over-the-Rhine.

Hudepohl emerged as the torchbearer of Cincinnati beer. The company bought the Burger brand in 1973. In order to compete in a market that was being encroached by imported beer, Hudepohl revived the brand name Christian Moerlein to produce a craft beer that became the first American beer to pass Germany's Reinheitsgebot purity law, in 1983. Christian Moerlein was a hit, but Hudepohl struggled in a market that was becoming dominated by the megabreweries. Hudepohl and Schoenling merged in 1986 but were still small in comparison to the national breweries that were eroding generations of local brand loyalty with multimillion-dollar ad campaigns. Finally, in 1991, Hudepohl-Schoenling outsourced its brewing operations to out-of-town owners. For a while, authentically Cincinnati beer was dead.

Although a number of Over-the-Rhine breweries temporarily returned after Prohibition, they did so without returning the neighborhood's original culture or vibrancy. Too many years had lapsed, too much had changed and the anti-German stigma of World War I lingered for years after the war. It only started to fade as the Nazis began a rise of power that would taint everything German in a whole new way. While they created jobs and produced good local beer, the post-Prohibition breweries also had very little impact on stopping the physical and socioeconomic decline of Over-the-

Rhine. It continued to become more impoverished and suffer widespread disinvestment. Hudepohl moved all of its brewing operations out of the neighborhood in 1958, just a year after Red Top, leaving only the McMicken office that it closed in 1967.

In 2006, the National Trust for Historic Preservation placed Over-the-Rhine on its list of the nation's Eleven Most Endangered Historic Places. It did so both due to the neighborhood's significance as well as its threatened status. Around the same size as New Orleans's French Quarter; containing most of the same architectural styles that compose Charleston's historic district; possessing the largest collection of nineteenth-century brewery buildings in the nation; home to Music Hall, Ohio's oldest farmers' market and numerous spectacular churches; and composed of a nationally unprecedented collection of three- to five-story, mixed-use, nineteenth-century tenement housing stock, Over-the-Rhine is one of the most significant and physically spectacular historic districts in the United States. However, this neighborhood with such a storied past, this place that could be the key to the city's revitalization, is being lost. In the five years prior to the National Trust's designation, fifty-two historic buildings were razed, and just between the 2006 designation and 2010, at least another fifteen have been destroyed. In a few years, Over-the-Rhine loses more historic buildings than those that compose entire coveted historic districts in other cities. During 2010, the neighborhood surpassed the loss of over 50 percent of the historic building stock that existed when Over-the-Rhine emerged from Prohibition. Even the neighborhood's remaining brewing history is threatened. On January 8, 2010, the nineteenth-century Christian Moerlein barrelhouse caught fire, quickly burning through the roof and shooting flames over one hundred feet into the air. Due to insurance and good ownership, the building will be saved, but the original location of the Hamilton Brewery was less fortunate. Although it had been unsympathetically modified in recent decades, the original exterior walls of the 1845 Hamilton Brewery remained under a layer of eroding stucco on the corner of Stonewall and McMicken. In late April 2010, after years of water intrusion from a leaking roof, the western wall started to bow and a large section collapsed. There were efforts to save it, but damage got worse in intervening days. The City of Cincinnati demolished the structure as an emergency measure less than a month later.

The good news for Over-the-Rhine's physical and cultural history is that there are people dedicated to saving it, rebuilding it and telling

The building in the foreground was believed to be the oldest remaining brewery building in the city of Cincinnati, constructed about 1845. Its broad, Italianate cornice work was probably added in the mid- to late nineteenth century. In addition to being the site of a raid by federal officials during Prohibition, this brewery complex was also the second to last of the original breweries to be used for commercial brewing operations in Over-the-Rhine, closing down under Red Top Brewing Company ownership in 1957.

the neighborhood's story. In 2005, members of the Brewery District Community Urban Redevelopment Corp. started promoting and marketing the northern half of Over-the-Rhine as the city's historic brewery district. Due to proximity to the canal, the ability to dig felsen tunnels back into the McMicken hillside and greater availability of land in a neighborhood that primarily grew from south to north, the majority of Over-the-Rhine and the West End's breweries were built north of Liberty Street. Most of the significant breweries that existed south of Liberty have been demolished, including the Gambrinus Stock Brewery (now a parking lot and a parking garage, with one horse stable remaining as a rehab facility), the Gerke Brewery (now a mirrored glass office building and surface parking lot at the corner of Central Parkway and Plum Street), the Banner Brewing Company (now the Emery building) and the Park Brewery (closed, razed and replaced with an apartment building at the corner of Thirteenth and Race in the 1890s). The vast majority of physical remains of the pre-Prohibition period

What is believed to have been the city's oldest brewery building suffered bad "modernization" work in the decades following its use as a brewery, but the original roofline and window openings could be seen under the stucco façade, cinderblock top addition and blocked-in and modified windows. Due to long-term neglect of its roof, the western wall began to collapse on April 18, 2010. More of the wall subsequently fell, and the building was razed as an emergency demolition by the City of Cincinnati in May 2010.

of Cincinnati brewing reside in the "Brewery District." Just establishing the name and identity of this area was a difficult task. Even some historic preservationists referred to the neighborhood's historic brewery buildings as "old industrial buildings," seemingly of lower importance than the residential structures. In the intervening years, and with a great deal of work by neighborhood proponents, this has changed. The Brewery District Community Urban Redevelopment Corp. (CURC) organized its first "Prohibition Resistance" tours of historic brewing sites in 2006. Organizers were skeptically questioned who would want to take tours of Over-the-Rhine, but hundreds of people did take the sold-out tours in 2006, leading to expansion in the following years. Under the organization of Brewery District CURC president Steven Hampton, additional versions of the tours are being offered in 2010 in an attempt to meet demands.

Bockfest, the annual celebration of Over-the-Rhine's German heritage, brewing history, bock beer and the coming of spring, has grown dramatically in the past several years. The festival is becoming a regional event that helps tell and promote the story of Over-the-Rhine's origins. Festival organizers have also been building relationships with German-American societies to help celebrate their Over-the-Rhine roots and revive traditional Sunday Gemütlichkeit.

Major strides are also occurring on the preservation and redevelopment fronts. Considerable public and private dollars have been invested to transform previously threatened buildings in the southern portion of the neighborhood into redeveloped housing, and 2010 marks the beginning of revitalization of Washington Park, work that will restore the beauty of Cincinnati's oldest public park for the residents of Over-the-Rhine and downtown. In October 2009, upon motion of Vice Mayor Roxanne Qualls, the city also created two volunteer task forces charged with making findings and recommendations that should dramatically improve the City of Cincinnati's approach to historic preservation and will hopefully lead to a loan program that can make redevelopment of deteriorating historic properties feasible for hundreds more would-be urban pioneers. In 2010, the neighborhood remains troubled. Hundreds of buildings remain vacant and over seventy are condemned, but if the hard work of the neighborhood's advocates is supported, Over-the-Rhine can rediscover and finally celebrate a rich, proud history that was lost when the nation entered World War I.

The most symbolic sign of Over-the-Rhine's rebirth is the physical return of its brewing heritage. In 2004, Greg Hardman, president and CEO of Christian Moerlein Brewing, bought the fledgling Christian Moerlein brand, Hudepohl, Schoenling, Burger and several other pre- and post-Prohibition beer brands. Since then, he has been reinventing these brands, returning the highest quality to the Moerlein name, bringing back Burger and a new Hudepohl 14-K. OTR Ale is a pale ale inspired by the best qualities of German beer made in Over-the-Rhine in the pre-lager period, and the names and packaging of the Moerlein brand celebrate the neighborhood's rich history. More importantly, when Hardman bought the city's most important historic beer brands, he had a vision of reconnecting these beers with Over-the-Rhine in more substantive ways than labels. As he grew the solvency of the company, improved quality and relaunched lost brands, he began looking for a new home for the company, a place in Over-the-Rhine that would let him return Christian Moerlein and Hudepohl to their origins.

After many months of complicated negotiations and a comedy of errors, with a lot of help from advisers, friends and partners, Hardman closed a deal on the last possible contract extension date of March 31, 2010, to buy a building that will be functioning as the new Hudepohl-Schoenling Brewery by 2011. Better known to many Cincinnatians as the former Husman Potato Chip factory, the building at 1621 Moore Street in Over-the-Rhine is largely composed of the original Kauffman Brewery. Hudepohl, the last commercial brewery to leave Over-the-Rhine, will become the brewery that restores regional commercial brewing to the neighborhood—just a couple of blocks removed from where Hudepohl began. According to plans, the lagering tunnels that remained sealed during decades of previous ownership will eventually be opened to the public. Portions of the nineteenth-century brewery will become a tasting room, and the facility will contain space memorializing Cincinnati's brewing history. Over-the-Rhine will never be what it once was, nor should it be; it was crowded, noisy, smelled bad and you could cut the air with a knife. But people like Greg Hardman, Steven Hampton and dozens of others who dedicate an amazing amount of their time, energy and effort to preserving and celebrating Over-the-Rhine's history believe that the neighborhood's past is the key to Cincinnati's future. Neither the injustices of the anti-German hysteria nor decades of socioeconomic decline can be reversed by drinking beer brewed in Over-the-Rhine, but it is a delicious place to start.

BIBLIOGRAPHY

Act Incorporating the City of Cincinnati and the Ordinances of Said City Now In Force. Cincinnati: Morgan, Fisher & L'Hommedieu, 1828.

Appel, Susan K. "Buildings and Beer: Brewery Architecture of Cincinnati." *Queen City Heritage: Journal of the Cincinnati Historical Society* 44, no. 2. Cincinnati, OH: Cincinnati Historical Society, September 1986.

Barry, John M. *The Great Influenza: The Epic Story of the Deadliest Plague in History.* New York: Penguin Books, 2005.

Billigheimer v. State. 32 O.S. 435.

Cincinnati Commercial. "Common Labor on Sunday," April 15, 1878.

———. "German Meetings," March 18, 1878.

———. "Sunday Laws to Be Enforced," April 7, 1878.

———. "Sunday in the Paris of America," April 2, 1878.

The Cincinnati Directory for the Year 1829. Cincinnati, OH: Robinson and Fairbank, 1829.

Cincinnati Post. "Children of Germans Oust Kaiser's Books," October 6, 1917.

———. "3,600 New Cases of Spanish Flu," October 12, 1918.

Cincinnati v. Rice. 15 O. 225 (1845).

Commercial Gazette. "The Children Can Drink It in Quantities with Perfect Safety: The Brewers Ahead," April 2, 1878.

Daily Enquirer. "A City in Arms, Mob Law Triumphant," April 5, 1855.

———. "German Man Attacked," April 6, 1855.

———. "The Main Law Passed," April 6, 1855.

————. "Mob Violence—Riots, the Mayor Severely Injured, Man Dangerously, if Not Fatally Stabbed," April 3, 1855.

————. "Outrage Upon Outrage—Another Ballot Box Destroyed by a Mob," April 4, 1855.

————. "Pap Taylor—The Mayor," April 9, 1855.

————. "Peace Once More," April 6, 1855.

————. "The Results—Its Consequences," April 3, 1855.

Dannedaum, Jed. *Drink and Disorder: Temperance Reform in Cincinnati from the Washington Revival to the WCTU.* Urbana and Chicago: University of Illinois Press, 1984.

Dobbert, Guido Andre. "The Disintegration of an Immigrant Community: The Cincinnati Germans, 1870–1920." PhD diss., University of Chicago, 1965.

Downard, William L. "Cincinnati Brewing Industry, 1811–1933: A Social and Economic History." PhD diss., Miami University, 1969.

Ermston, Judge. "Law Defiers: Plain Talk to the Saloonists by Judge Ermston." *Evening Post,* July 29, 1889.

Evening Post. "The 500 Aroused," July 26, 1889.

————. "A Friendly Word," July 27, 1889.

————. "Law to Be Upheld," July 27, 1889.

————. "More Censure: The Saloonkeepers' Association Sits Down on Its Turner Hall Brethren," August 8, 1889.

————. "Mosby Admonished," July 27, 1889.

————. "No Sunday Amusements," August 14, 1889.

————. "Saloonists Downed," July 29, 1889.

————. "Sunday Arrests," August 20, 1889.

————. "To Keep Open," July 26, 1889.

————. "Yesterday the Cincinnati Saloonkeepers' Rebellion Against Ohio Passed into a New Phase…," July 29, 1889.

————. "Yesterday 138 Saloonists of Cincinnati Inaugurated the Saloonists Rebellion," July 29, 1889.

Flack, Irwin. "Who Governed Cincinnati?" PhD diss., University of Pittsburgh, 1977.

F.L. Emmert Company papers, Box 1, Folder 1, Folder 4, Cincinnati Museum Center.

Foraker, Joseph Benson. *Notes of a Busy Life.* Cincinnati, OH: Stewart & Kidd Co., 1916.

Fort Wayne Weekly Gazette. "Berner Paroled: The Man Who Was the Cause of the Big Cincinnati Riot," June 6, 1895.

Gordon v. State (1889). 46 O.S. 607.

Grayson, Frank Y. *Pioneers of Nightlife on Vine St.* Cincinnati, OH: 1924.

Hamilton County Recorder, Deed Book 1234, p. 630.

———, Deed Book 1055, p. 600.

———, Deed Book 1958, p. 287.

———, Deed Book 1060, p. 457.

———, Deed Book 1063, p. 492.

Higham, John. *Strangers in the Land: Patterns of American Nativism 1860–1925.* New York: Antheneum, 1966.

Holian, Timothy J. *Over the Barrel: The Brewing History and Beer Culture of Cincinnati, Volume One, 1800–Prohibition.* St. Joseph, MO: Sudhaus Press, 2000.

Johnson, John A. *On the Roof of Europe: Behind the Guardsman's Rifle: The Cincinnati Riot of 1884.* Covington, KY: self-published, 1920.

Kempton, William D. *Kempton's Illustrated Vest Pocket Guide to Cincinnati and Vicinity.* Cincinnati, OH: W.D. Kempton, 1892.

Klauprecht, Emil. *Cincinnati, or, The Mysteries of the West.* Translated by Steven Rowan, edited by Don Heinrich Tolzman. New York: Peter Lang, 1996, originally published 1854.

———. *German Chronicles in the History of the Ohio Valley and Its Capital City Cincinnati in Particular.* Translated by Dale V. Lally Jr., edited by Don Heinrich Tolzmann. Bowie, MA: Heritage Press, 1992.

Laws and General Ordinances of the City of Cincinnati. Cincinnati, OH: Gazette Steam Printing House, 1859.

Laws and General Ordinances of the City of Cincinnati. Cincinnati, OH: R. Clarke, 1866.

Laws and General Ordinances of the City of Cincinnati. Cincinnati, OH: 1883.

Laws and General Ordinances of the City of Cincinnati. Cincinnati, OH: 1887.

Laws of Ohio, Vol. 29, p. 161, Sec. 1, 2, and 7 (1831).

———, Vol. 80, p. 167, Sec. 9 (1883).

———, Vol. 83, p. 160 (1886).

———, Vol. 85, p. 260 (1888).

———, Vol. 103, p. 222, Sec. 19 (1913).

———, Vol. 103, p. 224, Sec. 24 (1913).

Matthews, T.S. *Name and Address.* New York: Simon & Schuster, 1960.

Miller, Zane L. *Boss Cox's Cincinnati: Urban Politics in the Progressive Era*. New York: Oxford University Press, 1968.

Mosby, John papers, Box 1, Folder 3 and Box 8, Folder 6, Cincinnati Museum Center.

Oberlag, Lee. *Brewing in Cincinnati: 100 Years Hudepohl Brewing Company*. Cincinnati, OH: Hudepohl Brewing Company, 1983.

Ohio Revised Code, Sec. 6944, 7032a and 7034 (1886).

———, Sec. 7023a, 7033, 6940, 6942, 6943, 8092-8, 8092-18, 8092-22, 8092-33, 8092-35 (1890).

Ohio v. Foucar (1910), 8 O.L.R. 317.

Okrent, Daniel. *Last Call*. New York: Scribner, 2010.

Piqua v. Zimmerman (1875), 35 O.S. 507.

Schaffer's Advertising Directory for 1836–37. Cincinnati, OH: Truman & Smith, 1836.

Schaffer's Advertising Directory for 1839–40. Cincinnati, OH: Truman & Smith, 1839.

Shaw, James, Rev. *History of the Great Temperance Reform of the Nineteenth Century, Exhibiting: the evils of intemperance, the methods of reform, the woman's crusade, and the coming conflict of the temperance question*. Cincinnati, OH: Hitchcock & Walden, 1875.

Star, Stephen Z. "Prosit!! A Non-Cosmic Tour of the Cincinnati Saloon." *Festschrift for the German-American Tricentennial Jubilee*. Cincinnati, OH: Cincinnati Historical Society, 1982.

State v. Frame (1883), 39 O.S. 399.

State v. Hipp (1882), 38 O.S. 199.

Stevenson, Samuel. *Cincinnati in the Pocket*. Cincinnati, OH: Ira D. Dresser & Co., 1879.

Tolzmann, Don Heinrich. *The German American Experience*. New York: Humanity Books, 2000.

Tunison, J.S. *The Cincinnati Riot: Its Causes and Results*. Cincinnati, OH: Keating & Co. Printing, 1868.

Williams' Cincinnati Directory and Business Advertiser for 1850–51, and 1855, 1856, 1857, 1860, 1865, 1870, 1875, 1878, 1880, 1884, 1889, 1890, 1898, 1900, 1905, 1906, 1912, 1914.

Wimberg, Robert J. *Cincinnati Breweries*. Cincinnati: Ohio Book Store, 1989.

Wright, Henry C. *Bossism in Cincinnati*. Cincinnati, OH: 1905.

ABOUT THE AUTHOR

Michael Morgan is a reformed lawyer who has dedicated the past several years to the physical and cultural restoration of Cincinnati's Over-the-Rhine. In part, this includes working with the City of Cincinnati to improve its approach to historic preservation and to find creative solutions to urban redevelopment challenges. It also includes conducting events that help bring the neighborhood's  history alive. Morgan is a graduate of the University of Toledo College of Law, where he learned to write, and Ohio University, where he learned to drink. As a trustee of the Brewery District CURC, Morgan helped create the organization's Prohibition Resistance Tours of historic brewery sites. He has also been the primary organizer of Bockfest since 2006 and is an unabashed proponent of local beer.

Visit us at
www.historypress.net